the total at 22.

Chappell pushed forward to a ball from Lever and snicked a simple catch to [...]ok his 23rd [...] [...]he series.

Fortunately, Stackpole and Ian Redpath were able to settle down and consolidate the Australian position.

Stackpole, a tenacious fighter as well as a vigorous stroke-player, adopted the aggressive role while Redpath was wisely content to provide the stability.

Stackpole began to hammer the England bowling and he hooked Lever to the deep fine leg boundary for six and later lofted Underwood over the long-on boundary and into the Members' Stand.

The pair had added 49 runs in 72 minutes when Redpath surrendered his wicket, leaving Australia 3-71.

Redpath was dismissed when he turned an Illingworth delivery and was cleverly caught by John Hampshire, moving to his right with his arm elongated, at backward short square leg.

Australia's position ha[...]

Mins	Fours
119	7
210	3
69	1
28	4
145	4
106	2
70	2
94	1
39	2
4	0
8	0

(ampshire)

ver) 299

W
3
2
0
3
1
1
0

Also available at all good book stores

9781785315329

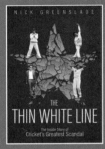

9781785317330

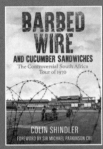

9781785316340

9781908051929

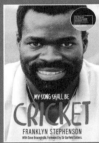

9781785315398

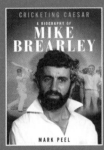

9781785316623

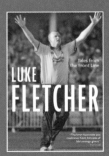

9781785316876

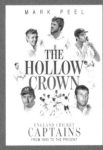

9781785316630

9781785316302

AND BRING THE DARKNESS HOME

Greg Milam

AND BRING THE DARKNESS HOME

The Tony Dell Story

First published by Pitch Publishing, 2021

Pitch Publishing
A2 Yeoman Gate
Yeoman Way
Worthing
Sussex
BN13 3QZ
www.pitchpublishing.co.uk
info@pitchpublishing.co.uk

A CIP catalogue record is available for this book
from the British Library.

ISBN 978 1 78531 851 1

Typesetting and origination by Pitch Publishing
Printed and bound in India by Replika Press Pvt. Ltd.

Contents

Acknowledgements

THIS BOOK would not exist without Tony Dell's willingness to tell his story. His openness and honesty, especially about the dark and difficult times, pointed the way. Sometimes gruff, sometimes cheery, he also put up with my interminable questions. With admirable frankness, his daughter Genevieve filled in many of the memory blanks in the family story, some of which had clearly been painful to her, her siblings and her mother. Sally Hodder proved a thoughtful eyewitness to the Tony Dell of today and the arc of his life.

Many of those who were there at points along the way were generous in offering their insights: Greg Delaney, Bruce Tanner, Ross Johnston, John George, Kevin Allcock, Sir Angus Houston, Peter Buchanan, Greg Chappell and Ken Eastwood. I am grateful to them all for their time and patience.

I am also thankful to the proper writers I know, my neighbour Romalyn Tilghman and my old buddy Kate Laven, for their wise counsel and relentless encouragement.

My wife Heather drives all the good in my life and her support and creativity, even on the brink of giving birth to our daughter, confirms her in my eyes as superhuman.

The idea for this book was given to me by the man who also gave me my first full-time paid job in journalism. I owe my career to Pat Symes and I will be forever grateful for his belief in me and the enduring power of a great story. This book is the result.

Introduction

FEW OF those listening to the BBC's *Test Match Special* during the Lord's Test in May 2018 will have been familiar with the life story of the guest interviewee during the tea break. Host Jonathan Agnew introduced Tony Dell as the man who once opened the bowling with Dennis Lillee and was the only living Test cricketer to have seen active military service.

It was a tantalising trailer for an interview that went on to reveal much about Dell's life in cricket and beyond. The talk of his work with fellow sufferers of post-traumatic stress disorder struck a particular chord at a time when society was wrestling with a growing global mental health crisis.

The interview also left lingering questions. In a sport so consumed by its own history, and that of the tragedy of so many players who had gone to war, how could a man with such a unique story not be more well known?

Dell was the only Test cricketer to serve in the Vietnam War. Following the death of Arthur Morris in 2015, Dell was indeed the last surviving Test cricketer to have seen action in a major theatre of war.

The scars of that service were long-lasting and largely hidden from view and the cost was immense, not least the loss of large chunks of his memory of his cricket career. The result was that Dell sometimes retreated to some safe after-dinner-style one-liners – 'months in Vietnam was very good training to be in Ian Chappell's dressing room' – but there was a deeper and more complex story to be told.

The added quirk that Dell fought in a war in the colours of Australia and played in the Ashes against England when he himself was still technically a 'Pom' was too much to resist.

Dell's family and friends, even Dell himself, admit he can be abrasive and impatient, a hard shell to crack. But there is also a compassion and kindness, especially to those veterans who have suffered far worse than him and who he feels have been abandoned. They have all been through so much.

Those who have seen combat at first hand will perhaps empathise with the words of Vietnam veteran Tim O'Brien, in his groundbreaking novel *The Things They Carried*: 'War is hell, but that's not the half of it, because war is also mystery and terror and adventure and courage and discovery and holiness and pity and despair and longing and love. War is nasty, war is fun. War is thrilling, war is drudgery. War makes you a man, war makes you dead.'

The title of this book is the last line of a poem by D.F. Brown. He served as a medic with the US Army in Vietnam in 1969 and 1970. He turned his experiences there into visceral and affecting verse on the chaos and horror of that war and the haunting, disorientating effect it had on its participants. In 2018 he told the *Houston Chronicle*: 'The last stress of my life is the fact that veterans are not being treated well.'

1

IT WAS, everyone could agree, no place to get lost. In the dead of night, in the depths of the jungle, at the very moment a bloody war was intensifying, the men of C Company of the 2nd Battalion of the Royal Australian Regiment were adrift in Vietnam.

What had started out as a routine patrol suddenly had the potential to become a massacre. Private Tony Dell, 22 years old and just a few days away from leaving the war zone of Vietnam for good, was one of them. So close to home he could almost smell it and yet now looking death in the face.

It should have been straightforward. As usual, soldiers nearing the end of their tour were given a mission close to their camp. This one: to prepare an ambush on a trail where, intelligence officers believed, communist forces would be tramping through to the village of Hoa Long. The Aussies, half a dozen of them, would be lying in wait. There was a protocol to follow, to head out in the late afternoon to a designated spot and wait for nightfall. 'That was the time the enemy was most likely to strike you,' Dell remembers.

Only, on this night, the corporal in charge got lost. As his men waited in the darkness, he set off to find the ambush point and came back empty-handed. He then tried and failed again. 'We got to the point where he just gave up and said, "Well, let's stay here the night and we'll go back to camp when the sun comes up."'

This was March 1968 and the Vietnam War was at a turning point. Just weeks earlier, the North Vietnamese had launched a surprise wave of attacks. The Tet Offensive brought assaults on a hundred cities in the south. It was to fail in military terms, the attacks repelled by South Vietnamese, American and Australian forces, but it did succeed in dramatically changing public opinion in the West about how well the war was going.

Instead of an enemy they had been told was fading, television viewers were shocked to see news coverage of a brazen counter-attack. Almost overnight, the questions about American and Australian involvement in the war became national debates. In February, Walter Cronkite, the journalist known as 'the most trusted man in America', had told his evening news viewers that he was 'more certain than ever that the bloody experience of Vietnam is to end in a stalemate'. Just as those back home were beginning to question the point of it all, the men of C Company 2nd Royal Australian Regiment were lost, slumped in the sweaty undergrowth of a pitch-black jungle night. 'We were all just higgledly-piggledy in the bush,' said Dell.

One of his fellow signallers in Vietnam that night had been at school with him in Brisbane a decade earlier. Corporal Kevin Alcock's assessment was blunt: 'They were late getting out there, late getting into position and were in the wrong place. They were stuck.'

Chapter 1

They all knew that only one thing could make matters worse.

'All of a sudden a hundred or so Viet Cong just walked through our position.'

The enemy they were sent to ambush – the People's Liberation Armed Forces of South Vietnam, the forces doing the bidding of communist North Vietnam in the south – had instead caught them unawares and unprepared. A comedy of errors in the jungle meant that one false move would have proved fatal for them all.

'We just had to shut up and hope like Christ no one spotted us,' said Dell. 'If someone coughed or if the bloody radio had squelched, we were goners.'

It was a moment – one of two from his time in Vietnam – that Private Dell would later identify as defining the story of the rest of his life. The 'abject fear' that would scar him for decades.

Each of those terrifying seconds felt like minutes. The only sound was the grinding of the Viet Cong soldiers' boots in the dirt and the clinking of the equipment they carried. Only those Aussies, trying hard to control their breathing, could hear the furious rushing sound of their blood in their ears. The prayers that their lives were not destined to end right there had to be silent. Kevin Alcock remembers Dell telling him: 'I was afraid they would hear my heart beat.'

'Unless you have been in that situation you have no idea what real fear is like,' Dell would tell a newspaper in 2013. 'I was absolutely shitting myself.'

There is the old cliché of life flashing before one's eyes in moments of deadly peril. But for that group of young men, sent to fight in a war that the world was now questioning, in that moment everything hung in the balance: lives to live, dreams to pursue, loves to share, families to raise. Even cricket to play. One sound, one turned head, and it was all over.

It lasted for the time it took those Viet Cong forces to pass by. And then, as quickly as they appeared, they were gone. Somehow the worst had not happened. The men of C Company had survived.

As signaller, it was Dell's job to fire up the radio and alert the artillery, to call in an attack on the Viet Cong column as it disappeared into the night. 'I tried to get on the radio and I was so shit-scared I couldn't talk.'

The memory of that night, recounted 50 years later from the comfort of his home in Queensland, has become a touchstone in the life of Tony Dell. By his mid-seventies, he had learned what that journey had cost him. In old age he had to work through experiences his younger self could never have fully understood, unravelling the strands and laying bare his vulnerabilities.

Only those who have seen combat at first hand can really tell of its true horrors. They are also the only ones who can really know what it left behind physically and emotionally. Perhaps they see something familiar in the thoughts of American soldier Frank Gabell. Returning from his service in World War Two, his home life had fallen apart. He wrote: 'War stinks! May all political and religious war-mongers be consigned to eternal hell.'

So many who made it through the war found they could not make it through the peace. For some, like Tony Dell, that was a private war that has lasted a lifetime.

By the time of the night of that near miss in March 1968, Tony Dell had been in Vietnam for ten months. He was serving in what was known as the ANZAC Battalion, made up of

Chapter 1

Australian and New Zealander infantry troops, the modern incarnation of the 'Diggers' who had fought alongside each other in World War One.

Dell had been plucked off the streets of Brisbane thanks to the controversial lottery system introduced by the Australian government to select conscripts for Vietnam. Young men were asked to sign a register in the year they turned 20. If their birth date was drawn, they were eligible for the call-up. It was one of the more unforgettable birthday gifts any government has ever handed its young citizens.

As it turned out, fewer than ten per cent of those eligible for National Service ended up getting the call. Tony Dell was one of the 15,000 'nashos' who went to Vietnam. 'It's the only lottery I've ever won,' he said. 'Pity it wasn't the one for $2m.'

Until that birthday ballot rudely interrupted life, Dell's focus had been on turning his promise as a club cricketer into something more substantial. Things were now set on a very different course. 'I guess at that stage I was pretty pissed off that I was one of the ones that had to go,' he said. Because the 'nashos' all shared a birthday, Dell and four others from Brisbane could arrange shared celebrations. On 5 August 1966, they all jumped in a Mini and set off from the base in Singleton in New South Wales, headed for home. At midnight they pulled up in the tiny parish of Glen Innes, jumped out of the car and celebrated their 21st together with a beer or four. Training had begun earlier that year. Within months Tony Dell would be bound for Vietnam. 'I was a ready-made soldier.'

To this day that war remains one of the most divisive in history. To many Vietnam is a byword for military misadventure overseas. The stuff of countless movies was very real in the middle of the 20th century. At the height of the Cold War, the United States was gripped by the fear that Soviet influence would topple countries like dominoes under the communist spell. When the colonial French were defeated by the Vietnamese communist revolutionary Ho Chi Minh, the alarm bells were ringing in Washington.

Driven by the fear of Ho's North Vietnam taking over the south, American involvement began in 1955, exploded into all-out conflict in 1965 and would end in ignominy in 1973. By the time communist forces did take control of South Vietnam, more than three million people had died. Half of those were Vietnamese civilians and some 58,000 were Americans.

For Australians, the fear of that domino theory was an existential one. Geography alone was a reason to look nervously towards South East Asia. When the call for full support came from US President Lyndon B. Johnson (known as LBJ), the Australian government responded enthusiastically. By the time the last Aussie soldier left Vietnam in 1972, 60,000 had seen service there, 3,000 were listed as wounded and 521 had been killed.

The full cost for those who made it home would take years to reveal itself.

In 1967, the country of Vietnam certainly held little to impress a new arrival from Brisbane. 'It was hot and it was wet. The soil was red. It was dusty when it was dry or boggy when it rained.' One of the few comforts in the jungle was the tubes of condensed milk sent from home by his mother, a delight he later remembered as 'almost edible'.

Chapter 1

He almost never made it to Vietnam at all. During predeployment jungle training in Australia, Dell was climbing down a rope with his full kit strapped to his back when he lost his grip and fell. His leg was broken – 'not a bad break' – and, because he had not fully completed his training, he says he was offered the chance to skip deployment to Vietnam altogether. The option of 12 months of mess duty and parades held little appeal, though. Dell said he would go to war.

Home was the camp at Nui Dat, 50 miles south-east of the South Vietnamese capital Saigon. It was a place that had already given Australian forces a taste of the ferocity of the fight.

The location for the base was chosen because it was right on the doorstep of the Viet Cong. So sympathetic to the communists were residents of the two nearest villages – Long Tan and Long Phuoc – that the Australian commander ordered the entire populations of both be removed. Some 4,000 people along with their livestock were resettled and the villages destroyed without compensation. It doomed any effort to win the hearts and minds of locals. Building a camp on a key Viet Cong supply route was also guaranteed to prompt an enemy response. It duly arrived.

For weeks in the summer of 1966, Australian military intelligence had been tracking the movement of the Viet Cong towards the remains of Long Tan. A force of 2,500 were thought to have assembled ready to attack Nui Dat. But every Australian patrol that went out to look for them drew a blank. On the night of 16 August, the Viet Cong announced their presence. The enemy bombardment of artillery and mortars, launched from a mile away, injured two dozen Australian men, one fatally.

In their pursuit of the Viet Cong forces the next day, a company of Australians barely 100 strong found themselves trapped and heavily outnumbered. As Viet Cong forces closed in for the kill, the men of D Company somehow held off a full assault until relief arrived. In the three days of fighting on that rubber plantation, 18 Australians died.

The story of the Battle of Long Tan would give rise to numerous controversies – not least over the wildly varying numbers of Viet Cong fighters who were killed – but it undoubtedly served as a warning for new arrivals that they were in for a fight, and that Nui Dat – literally translated as 'dirt hill' – was a hill men were willing to die for.

To a 21-year-old newcomer, life as a private had a familiar routine, shaped by the landscape of south-eastern Vietnam. Those plantations were dark and deadly places, offering the perfect cover and clear field of fire for an enemy hidden within. The rice paddies were no safer, open and exposed, and heavy going in the monsoon rains between May and October. 'I remember one night we had to "stop and prop". We had to spend the night in six inches of water,' says Dell. Changing clothes was a luxury: 'You might have a couple of pairs of socks because your feet were always wet but not much else.' Every evening would also bring the routine of removing the half a dozen or so leeches from some of the more delicate areas of the body. A lighted cigarette was found to be the most effective means.

Dell was sanguine about life at war. 'The more I got into it, the more it appealed to me. I thought, "Let's make the best of it." We were playing real soldiers. It was a boy's own adventure. In fact, my main memory of it was that I didn't mind it one little bit.'

Chapter 1

Dell's schoolfriend Greg Delaney remembers asking him about his first contact with the enemy in Vietnam. 'He said he dived behind a log and another bloke called Joe did the same and they came face to face. He said it was raining leaves from the bullets flying over the top of them. He and Joe was just inches apart and, he couldn't understand why, but they just laughed. Maybe it was sheer terror, but they just laughed.'

Being 6ft 5in tall had its advantages and its drawbacks. 'You're an easy target when you're such a tall bugger wandering through the jungle,' said John George, a lieutenant who would go on to became second-in-command of C Company. 'Luckily he had a great sense of humour about it.'

His height was more useful elsewhere. The battalion's official history reveals improvised games of cricket took place in between the lines of tents at Nui Dat. Years later, looking at an action photo of a group of his mates, stripped to the waist, with a plank for a bat and boxes for the stumps, Dell was perplexed. 'Seems we DID play cricket,' he said. 'A number of guys have told me since about facing me in the lines, but I don't remember.'

Camp life did offer some relief from the strain of combat. There were good-humoured hostilities inside Nui Dat over whose music should be played loudest. It was dubbed 'The war of the tape recorders', the Beatles versus Peter, Paul and Mary, and was eventually settled amicably, one soldier said, according to the rules of the Geneva Convention.

Attached to headquarters company as one of the two signallers, Private Dell's life was much like that of the thousands who served in Vietnam, governed by the search for an enemy more used to the surroundings. 'We would go out on search-

and-destroy missions, we would go through villages and you'd never know who was a normal villager and who might be Viet Cong by night. We'd be looking for weapons and they'd have these things stashed away. At night-time they'd get those out and do stuff with them.'

That 'stuff' was the insurgency they had been sent to counter. From the moment they embarked on their adventure in Vietnam, the Americans knew they had little experience of jungle warfare. They also knew the Australians and New Zealanders did have it. Both countries had fought alongside the British during the Malayan Emergency, a guerrilla war also fought in a landscape of plantations.

The first Australian involvement in Vietnam had been a small team of advisors sent to train Americans on the tactics they had learned in Malaya. Like the US though, the Australians would soon realise that those first few teams of advisors were never going to be enough. This was a conflict that would ultimately require thousands.

It was apparent to everyone on the ground that this was an uneven fight. On those ambushes, they set traps on trails identified as likely to be used by Viet Cong. Dell said: 'Sometimes we just felt they were there sitting watching us.'

It was on Australia Day, 26 January 1968, that the second of the incidents took place that would burn itself into the consciousness of a young soldier. He may not have known it at the time but it would haunt and shape the rest of Dell's life.

The men of C Company had been deployed to a province north-east of Saigon to support American and South Vietnamese forces preparing for that expected Tet Offensive. Operation

Chapter 1

Coburg was to cost 17 Australians, two New Zealanders and one American their lives.

In one assault, soldiers from C Company took on a bunker believed to contain as few as a dozen Viet Cong soldiers. They were wrong and what followed was a 17-hour ordeal as wave after wave of Viet Cong counter-attacks poured in and the Aussies clung on for life. The platoon commander later told a reporter: 'Our spotter plane flew over and told us there were thousands of them swarming towards us.' John George remembers that day clearly. 'I recall telling the sergeant major, "The rounds are ten feet high, the bastards can't shoot." With that a burst of machine-gun fire cut the bushes in front of us. The sergeant major pushed my head to the ground, fell on top of me and said: "They're not ten fucking feet high now."' That company sergeant major, in the eyes of George and Dell, saved many lives that day: 'Without Reg Jones we would have been fucked.'

During that attack Graham Norley, a 24-year-old corporal from Adelaide, was shot and killed as he was chatting with a colleague. John George remembers a sentry slumping next to him having been shot through the nose. As George wrestled with a field dressing and told the stricken soldier to lift up his hanging nose so he could bandage it in place, the soldier wondered aloud: 'What's my mother going to say about me not having a bloody nose?' Lt George summoned up the company medic, Private Jock Davison, to help remove the bloodied soldier from the firing line. Davison, 27 years old and on loan from another company, was shot and killed. Years later, George said: 'I blame myself for his death.'

They had lost others too. In September 1967, privates Leslie Weston and William Brett were killed alongside an interpreter in an ambush of their Land Rover at a checkpoint.

For Private Dell, the sudden and violent loss of comrades put the reality of death right in front of him. In the heat of battle, there is no time to stop and question the freak nature of why one lives and another dies, why one returns to his family on his own two feet but another is carried home in a box. There is no time to wonder either about the mental scars all of this will inflict. Those questions are for later.

And it was not the deaths of men on his own side that would cause the lasting nightmares for Tony Dell. In fact, decades later he remained matter of fact about it. 'It is sad that they're gone. It is the worst part of the job. But you get on with it.'

It wasn't meant to sound callous; his affection for his comrades had never dimmed. 'If you're in the army, especially if you're deployed in combat, there's nothing closer than the mates you had.'

Lt John George, a man who was to serve for a quarter of a century in the Australian Army, explained: 'I've had guys killed next to me. Look, you accept it as a soldier. It is a tragedy. It's upsetting. It happens. It is war. You can never let it get to you. You can't worry about it. If you're not focused, you could be next.'

For Dell it was deaths on the other side that would leave the scars. Like that brush with death as the Viet Cong tramped over their heads in the bush, to Dell's mind, the sight of dead enemy caused the lasting psychological damage. The aftermath during Coburg in a Viet Cong camp was particularly affecting.

Chapter 1

Forty years on, Dell's voice would become strained at the memory, the words trailing off. The gruesome reality of war: the backs of heads that had been blown off, brains splattered everywhere, soldiers shot in the chest and their backs exploded by the force of the round. He saw it all, more than once. 'You see all the blood and guts but it doesn't hit you until later. You see it everywhere. It doesn't affect you greatly at the time because it is part of the process. But it is a horrific sight.'

He would come to understand what it had done to him. Back then, he didn't have a clue. 'You're never able to process it because you've got a job to do. You just carry on. There's always another search and destroy to be done. The story was that there were thousands of North Vietnamese soldiers coming down the Ho Chi Minh trail to take over Saigon. You just have to get through it.'

It is a story that generations have told. The job that had to be done. No time to wallow in the fear or loss, certainly little chance to talk about that to your mates.

It is a different story to the one told in a documentary film released by the Australian military in 1968. The 30-minute film showed those back home what the 'Diggers in Vietnam' were up to. It was a 'complex and ever-changing environment of a strange war', the film cautioned, but it painted a picture of a reassuringly neat end to every day. Once the casualties had been mopped up and the enemy prisoners searched and refreshed with a kindly cigarette, when the 'diggers return to base, they'll talk over their experience with their mates, just as their fathers did in wars gone by, the things they did, the places they've seen'. Maybe those soldiers, their nervous smiles and eyes full of trepidation for the cameras, did talk things over on those long nights. That was not what Tony Dell remembered. 'My recollection is that there wasn't a great deal of discussion amongst us.'

According to the soothing voice on the film, being on the move in the jungle offered soldiers some respite from the nervous tensions of war. Far better than worrying about what dangers lurked in the shadows, it said, was to be out there actually confronting them for real. That way the physical problems outweigh the mental strain.

Any positive feeling on the ground had much to do with the story those young Australians had been told about the reasons for the war. If there was a civilian ambivalence back home, no one in authority was taking any chances with the mindset of the soldiers. 'It was drilled into you. You were going to fight the red peril. This was a time of "reds under the bed", the Cold War and all of that. There was the thought that the communist Chinese were going to march down through Vietnam and Indonesia and populate Australia. That was the theme. To a point we were brainwashed. By the time you had finished training, you hated them.'

It was the sort of mentality, he says, looking back from the distance of five decades, that would lead to war crimes in that conflict and elsewhere. 'It's not until you come home and hear a few truths and see what the rest of the world is saying that you have second thoughts about "should I have even been there?" I was just a private doing what I was told.'

His family, he said, had shown no animosity towards the authorities for dispatching him to war. A father who had joined the navy at 15 and found himself in World War Two five years

Chapter 1

later would have known a thing or two about service. His mother was not one of those to join the 'Save Our Sons' movement that filled Australia's newspapers. A picture on one front page showed a woman refusing to let go of her 20-year-old grandson as he awaited the troop train at Sydney Central. On the inside pages, organiser Joyce Golgerth told a reporter: 'These boys are healthy, strong, on the threshold of their lives and they could come home maimed, blinded or they could die in a war which has been described as a bottomless pit of violence and horror.'

As it was, the story of the Vietnam War was one of a slow dawning of reality, a gradual ebbing of belief and a realisation that many of those who survived it were scarred for life.

At least in the field there were efforts at maintaining morale. A unit newspaper was printed, named *Ringo* after the battalion march, and copies were hard to get hold of. Passed from man to man and sometimes sent to wives and girlfriends back home, the poems, stories and cartoons poked around in the dark humour of life at war.

To the tune of 'The Twelve Days of Christmas' were the lyrics for 'Twelve Months in Vietnam': 'On the first month in Vietnam, my CO said to me: A sniper in a bushy-topped tree.' So it went on. No geese a-laying, gold rings or calling birds, instead 'six sex-starved soldiers, five Hershey bars and four gunships gunning'.

Alongside the laughs though, readers might have swallowed hard at some of the truths told in *Ringo*. In particular, the poem 'Mates in Vietnam' was stark: 'It's hot, it's dark, it's eerie, it's calm. The VC jungles of Vietnam.' The fear pours out of every word. 'When suddenly your heart is thumping, the blood to your head swiftly pumping, your mouth is dry, your nerves are taut, for you've heard a sound that you should not.' The soldier-poet writes of opening fire on a Viet Cong fighter – 'You shoot twice more and watch him die' – but others have gone to ground.

> That awful feeling you had before
> Is returning more and more.
> I can't see them, can they see I?
> Please God above, don't let me die.
> When suddenly machine guns burst
> And above it, Aussie Diggers curse:
> 'We've got the bastards, don't worry mate.'
> But you don't hear, you say a prayer:
> 'Thank God above, my mates were there.'

There is no way of knowing how many men read those words, credited to the 'Gaspers Group', but they would hit home for those who did. They might very well still gnaw away in the minds of some of the thousands who were there.

'They went away as boys but came back as men,' said the narrator on that Australian government film, as pictures rolled of soldiers disembarking the troop ship HMAS *Sydney* on their return home. Much more had changed for many of them, invisible to the cameras or even the eyes of those family members who clamoured to hug and kiss them. What darkness they had brought back with them.

The battalion history book contains two photographs of Private Dell in Vietnam. In one, his hulking frame is perched on a stack of boxes, hunched and facing away from the camera. In the other, he is too tall to fit in the frame of the photo. As with any photo where the face is obscured, it has an elusive quality, a moment in time that tells some of a story but leaves so much more unsaid.

Another of Dell's schoolfriends, Bruce Tanner, remembers reading a letter he had sent from Vietnam. It told of 'blokes trying to kill you, you shooting back but you just can't stop them'. Tanner says now: 'It was so poignant. Here was this big, jovial, gregarious bloke we were used to seeing laughing all the time, and he was scared shitless.'

By the time he headed home to Australia – that moment soldiers in Vietnam called their 'wake-up' – Tony Dell had done his bit for his country. The battalion history gives us a list of the bald facts: 28 of 2RAR dead, 122 wounded. They add up the successes too: 2,648 pits and bunkers destroyed and, somewhat oddly, 11 ox carts put out of use.

But like the other 'nashos', there was no military unit for him to return to – it was straight back to civilian life. What he calls that transition story, as much as the horrors he confronted during that war, played a part in how his life unfolded. His mates in the jungle saw nothing in his behaviour to make them concerned for him but, then, they were all looking out for themselves too. How can anyone really know what is going on in the mind of another when it is hard enough to know what is going on in your own?

More than 40 years later, Tony Dell told a reporter: 'I saw things in Vietnam that the human brain is not meant to experience.' It had taken him decades to work through to that conclusion. His impression of service in that war, on landing back in Brisbane in 1968, was pointed but telling: 'I got home safely. Physically.'

2

ON A sunny, breezy Friday morning, less than three years after returning home from Vietnam, Tony Dell stood at the summit of sporting achievement. Twenty-five years old, he was about to make his debut for Australia against their oldest cricketing enemy. The Test match against England at the Sydney Cricket Ground would decide the Ashes series of 1970/71, the latest chapter in the sport's oldest contest.

In the week leading up to the match, Dell's face had filled the front and back pages. It was a sporting nation in desperate need of a new cricketing hero. The series had been a disappointment for the home crowd and Australia had to win that seventh and final game in Sydney to tie the series and retain the Ashes.

Dell's height seemed to especially excite the newspapers. On the front page of the *Sydney Sun-Herald* sports section was a photo of Dell, dressed in a suit, shirt and tie, hands reaching towards the camera, fingers spread, under the headline: 'The biggest grip in the game'. The story read: 'In these massive hands of Australia's new Test opening bowler Tony Dell, the fate of the Ashes could lie. He says he probably has the biggest hands in the game and as they measure nine inches few would argue.'

Hands aside, the selection of 'the cyclone from the north', as *The Age* in Melbourne dubbed him, was judged a risk. 'Giant paceman is a gamble for the Test', warned one headline. Another called him an unknown quantity, whose elevation was a 'silent prayer and a gamble' by selectors who felt desperate measures were necessary to salvage a miserable Australian summer. Not all of the coverage was so hopeless: 'Dell may or may not succeed. Whatever he does he is sure to be a prominent figure among Australian bowlers for many years to come,' wrote one correspondent.

He had been chosen largely on the back of a performance for his state Queensland against South Australia a month earlier. Remarkably, it was only his eighth match in first-class cricket but he did enough to catch the eye of a notable opponent. Barry Richards, one of the most sublime batsmen of his age, told reporters that Dell's 'first five or six overs are as good as I've seen and his bumper can be frightening'. The Australian cricket world sat up and took notice. Neil Harvey, a former Australian batting hero who had become national team selector, was at that game on the hunt for fresh talent. They wanted a fast bowler who could put the wind up the English batsmen – and Tony Dell was their man.

Greg Chappell can remember standing at the non-striker's end as Richards faced up to Dell. At 22, Chappell had been closely observing the South African legend that season, eager to learn everything he could from such a cricketing colossus. What he saw was Tony Dell causing problems for Richards. 'It was the only time I saw Barry's footwork change. He found him more awkward than most because of his height and the left-arm swing and bounce.' Even to two masters of the science and art of batting, the messages between hand and eye, tuned to the millisecond, could be thrown off by a bowler like Dell. 'You had to rewire the software,' said Chappell.

Remember, this is the same Barry Richards who, a month before facing Dell, had scored 325 in a day against a bowling attack including Dennis Lillee, Graham McKenzie and Tony Lock, three men who would clock up 180 Test caps between them. Greg Chappell saw Dell as offering Australia's bowling something different.

Cricket often enjoys the language of warfare to stir the spirits. The novelty of someone who had served his country in a real war stepping up in a sporting one did not go unnoticed. 'Dell knows all about the war zone,' wrote Phil Wilkins in the *Sydney Morning Herald*. 'When the hot lead starts flying at the Sydney Cricket Ground on Friday, he could be grateful for the experience. It promises to be better than the gunfight at the OK Corral.'

For years, Greg Chappell says, he had no idea that Tony Dell had been to war.

Dell was happy to play along as the warrior-cricketer ready to do battle again. He said his time in Vietnam had prepared him well for cricket's highest level. 'If I hadn't had to do two years' National Service, I don't think I would ever have had the chance to play Test cricket,' he said at the time. From the distance of decades, his next words seem prescient: 'A couple of years in the army changed my outlook on everything – life, cricket, people.'

The main benefit of his two years in the military was physical fitness. 'One of the perceived problems I had was that I wasn't fit enough for first-class cricket. I came back from Vietnam and in one of my first games back I bowled all afternoon and got seven wickets. So, I guess I was fitter after I came back.'

When Tony Dell returned from the war in March 1968, some things resumed as if he had never been away. Civilian employers were required by law to keep open the jobs of National Servicemen. Dell picked up where he had left off as an advertising media manager in Brisbane.

The enforced interruption to his cricket career had been a frustration. In quiet moments under canvas in Vietnam, he would listen to cricket reports on the radio. Like the letters from home, they would update him on the progress of players who had been his contemporaries before the war. Queensland was trying out bowlers left, right and centre and there was Dell stuck in the army in a far-off jungle. It irritated him.

When the new cricket season arrived at the end of 1968 then, his first since returning home from war, he felt it was his turn to step up to the big time. He impressed in a match for the Queensland Colts against New South Wales. But still the phone call from the state selectors didn't come.

They may have been swayed by another damaging perception of Dell. A newspaper column, its writer anonymous, put it bluntly: 'He was fast all right – I know, I faced him in several games in Brisbane. But he was also unruly in character and rather reluctant to devote himself to the work needed to make the grade.' Whatever the reason, Dell would spend a frustrating two more years in club cricket.

He was living in a flat in Lisburn Street in East Brisbane, a stone's throw from the Gabba, the ground that was the home of Queensland cricket. His social life centred on Brisbane's Embassy

Hotel, across the street from his work and the spiritual birthplace of the rugby team that would feed his other sporting passion.

All the time, the war in Vietnam continued to rage and Australians continued to die. Shortly after Dell came home, he received sobering news from the front line. Johnny Fraser had been a schoolboy sporting legend in Brisbane, a promising cricketer and rugby player, a stellar student with expectations of a glittering career ahead of him. Then his number came up in that National Service lottery. 'He was a bloke we all admired, all looked up to,' Dell said. Fraser was selected for officer training and commissioned as a second lieutenant. Just when it looked like he had avoided deployment to Vietnam he was sent to the war zone.

In March 1968, Fraser was commanding a platoon on an operation to clear caves that had been mined and booby trapped by the Viet Cong. As they edged their way towards a cave entrance, Fraser triggered an anti-personnel mine. They referred to them as 'jumping jacks'. Step on one and it would shoot four feet into the air before detonating, exploding shrapnel in all directions, at waist height, calculated to do maximum possible damage. When Johnny Fraser realised he had triggered the mine, he used his body to smother it as best he could.

Pat Burgess, a war correspondent for the *Sydney Morning Herald*, was with Fraser's platoon at the time. 'As the dust of the exploding mine began to settle,' he wrote, 'a voice echoed in the gully above the cries of the other wounded: "Don't come in for me, don't come in. There's more there."' When a helicopter arrived to evacuate the casualties, Burgess wrote: 'The first Digger, the worst wounded, swung up first, lying very still in the basket. It was Johnny Fraser, the National Serviceman with the gap-toothed, ever-ready grin.'

Burgess sat drinking tea with Johnny's closest friend in Vietnam, a soldier also called Fraser. Peter Fraser was no relation but the two were like brothers: 'In the showers in Sydney it was the two Frasers who had led the singing of their version of the ballad "There Won't Be Many Coming Back".'

Burgess heard a voice calling them on the radio. 'Peter picked up the handset, listened and said "Johnny's dead". He walked behind a boulder and squatted there, and the rest of the platoon gradually deliberately moved away so that he was quite alone. Down the yellow and grey dirt, tears on the face of young Peter Fraser made muddy smudge marks like those on a young boy's face.'

Johnny Fraser was the only soldier to die in that incident. His actions saved the lives of others around him. He was 23 years old. The headline to Burgess's account of his death harked back to that battalion song: 'Johnny won't be coming back.'

His death was a shattering blow back home, especially to another young National Serviceman, fresh back off the boat from Vietnam and who had idolised Fraser for his heroics during their schooldays in Brisbane. Fraser was buried with full military honours in the town of Nerang on Queensland's Gold Coast. Tony's friend Greg Delaney remembers: 'The first week of Tony being home I took him to John's funeral and I think all of that messed him up quite a bit.'

Dell says simply: 'It was quite confronting.'

A park close to where Fraser grew up in Surfers Paradise, where he played and fished as a child, is now named in his memory.

The news of death had kept on coming. Days before Fraser's loss, three soldiers died when mines detonated close to Dell's old base at Nui Dat. He was thousands of miles from Vietnam by then, outwardly living the life of those who had never gone to war, the life he had enjoyed before his service. But Vietnam – the deaths, the protests, the politics, the homecomings – was the background noise in every Australian's life, something that was impossible to ignore.

It affected some more than others – even if it would take more than 40 years to discover the damage the darkness had left behind.

For now, in his early twenties and back home in Brisbane, life for Dell was all about work and cricket. After Queensland finally recognised Dell as being good enough for a shot at first-class cricket in 1970, the elevation to international cricket came quickly.

'I'll admit it, it knocked me completely sideways,' he said of his Test selection at the time. A reporter had phoned asking for some personal details. 'He said he was almost certain I was in the Test side. I told him, for Pete's sake, to find out for sure, that I couldn't bear the tension.' The reporter phoned back to confirm the news. 'I tell you I was shaking when I put the phone down.'

Just as thrilled was his cricket-mad dad Ross. Dell was asked if he had phoned his father to tell him the news of the call-up. 'No,' replied Dell, 'he phoned me.' Dell senior would cancel a business trip to Japan to ensure he was there for his son's debut. Johnny Green, Dell's boss at the advertising agency, was an old friend of Ross Dell and poked fun at his enduring loyalty to England. 'I said to him one day: the day will come when your son will be bowling for Australia out there and I will be sitting right beside you,' Green remembered.

The day did come. Dell's schoolfriend Greg Delaney also remembers hearing the news. He was at Tattersall's, then a men-only sporting club in Brisbane, when Dell's selection was announced over the public address system. 'About 20 minutes later I was paged. I answered the call and it was Tony. I congratulated him and he said, "I'm coming up there, you'll get in the car with me, I want to see your old man today."' Years before Delaney's father had watched the pair play cricket as teenagers on his lawn. 'He loved Tony and I remember him yelling out to him, "You're going to play for Australia one day."' Dell had never forgotten those words. 'He wanted to see my dad first. It was a lovely thing and dad was obviously very moved by it.'

In many ways Dell's call-up was remarkable. He had only made his senior debut for Queensland in October of 1970. To be picked for the national side by February 1971 was a meteoric rise. That the men who picked him included Sir Donald Bradman, widely regarded as the greatest batsman of all time, put an extra spring in the step of the young fast bowler. Bradman's selections for that Test were to be his last. Controversially, the captain Bill Lawry was dropped – the only time in Australia's history that a captain had been removed during a series – and the bowling attack was the most inexperienced since cricket had resumed after World War Two.

Of new captain Ian Chappell's front-line bowlers, Dell had never played a Test match, while Dennis Lillee, Terry Jenner and Kerry O'Keefe had played one each. Two other future giants of Australian cricket, Greg Chappell and Rodney Marsh, had also made their debuts in that Ashes series. Against this green line-up, England were a gritty and experienced bunch led by Ray Illingworth.

Illingworth had been far from complimentary about the opponents' new fast left-arm bowler before the match. 'He is lively for about six overs, but after that I don't think we will have much to fear. I must say I would like to bat against him after he had sent down 30 overs.' Illingworth's review will have been informed by one of the handful of games Dell had played up to that point, for Queensland against the English tourists in Brisbane in November. The local press certainly gave him a big build-up for the match. 'He is the Atlas of the summer game here,' wrote one cricket correspondent. As the only left-arm opening bowler in Australian first-class cricket at the time, he was already being touted as an international prospect. But there were doubts. Was he a 'four-over wonder'? Did he have enough 'tiger'? There was also the not-inconsiderable fact that he had yet to actually take a wicket in his career. He pointed to a dozen dropped catches off his bowling and, although he had still failed to claim a victim in that England match, the Test selectors saw enough. Dell was picked for the Test side, the real deal with the Ashes at stake.

It had been 90 years since the two countries first competed for that small urn of dust. The story of the Ashes is familiar to every cricket fan. When England suffered their first home defeat to Australia in 1882, a mock obituary appeared in the *Sporting Times*: 'In Affectionate Remembrance of English Cricket,' it went, 'the body will be cremated and the ashes taken to Australia.' When England headed to Australia a few months later, captain

Chapter 2

Ivo Bligh promised to bring back 'the Ashes of English cricket'. After England's victory at the Sydney Cricket Ground, a group of Melbourne ladies burned a bail, sealed the ashes in an urn and presented it to the victorious Bligh. There have been some titanic struggles for symbolic possession of the Ashes ever since.

At the start of the 1970/71 series, Australia held them. But a thumping defeat at Sydney in the fourth match had given England the upper hand. It had not been one of the most thrilling of Ashes contests, with four matches drawn and one washed out by rain without a ball being bowled. By the time the seventh and final Test rolled around, only victory for the new-look young Australian team would ensure a drawn series and the Ashes remaining in their hands.

To the cricket watcher of today, it might seem like the game back then was played in an alien world. In Australia they still played eight-ball overs, only the final session of the day was televised live and Test matches featured a rest day. The concept of international limited-overs cricket was almost unheard of. In fact, that washed-out Test in Melbourne led to the birth of one-day international cricket. A 40-overs-per-side game was arranged for the last scheduled day of the match and a crowd of 46,000 came to watch Australia win comfortably. What was a novelty then was to become a regular fixture of international cricket within a few years. Within half a century, it had come to dominate.

For Tony Dell that seventh Test meant one thing: 'All of a sudden, I'd arrived.'

Another Australian was making his debut in that Test, too. Ken Eastwood, a 35-year-old opening batsman who had not even been able to get into his state side at the start of the season, was as much of a surprise call-up as Dell. He remembers a shambolic build-up to the pair's big day – the lack of organisation, he said, amazed him. There was no one to meet him at the airport, no team meetings, and Eastwood even had to pay a visit to a sports shop in the city to pick up his team sweater. They only had sleeveless. He would finally get his long-sleeved one and his official blazer nearly a year later. Most shambolic of all, he said, the taxis that the captain Ian Chappell had ordered for the short drive from the team's motel in Woollahra to the Sydney Cricket Ground failed to turn up. Eastwood remembers: 'Terry Jenner, who was a car salesman away from cricket, said, "Come on, we'll get our own taxi." We got out on to the main road and he starts hitch-hiking. Hitch-hiking to the Test match. A bloke pulls up on his way to work and Terry, who could talk underwater, gets him to take us to the ground.' Jenner and Eastwood made it to the ground on time, and the lucky driver decided to ditch work for a day at the cricket instead. 'It was unbelievable,' said Eastwood. He also had no idea that his fellow debutant had been to war.

Dell's memory of that week is nowhere near as pin sharp as Eastwood's. There was confusion about a sweater, yes, and no hotel had been booked for the night before the match. He stayed at the flat of Greg Chappell and his girlfriend. Other than those snippets, Dell remembers very little of that momentous occasion. There are just the odd flashes of memories, snatches of the match, impressions and senses. A shame. He would come to learn the reason why much later.

By chance that seventh Test would turn out to be one of the most controversial in cricket, not just Ashes, history.

Chapter 2

There was still time for fate to almost scupper Dell's international dream. He suffered a back injury in the build-up to the Test. There were doubts over whether he could be risked. In those days, players were sent letters warning them of the dangers of concealing an injury likely to affect the team. Dell was eventually passed fit.

A bigger worry in the build-up to the match was the state of the pitch. Six inches of rain had fallen in 12 days and the wicket had been covered for 36 hours before the start of play. 'It has been freely expressed that this Test will be a bowlers' picnic with the ball flying dangerously from a lush wicket,' warned the *Herald*. England's 'professional band of bowlers' would delight in an under-prepared pitch. And Australia's giant debutant should have been licking his lips when his captain won the toss and decided to bowl first. Tony Dell's moment of cricketing truth had arrived.

England were bowled out before the end of the first day's play. Dell, opening the bowling with Lillee, removed England veterans John Edrich and Basil D'Oliveira. But surprisingly on that green wicket, it was the spinners Jenner and O'Keefe who did most of the damage. Bill O'Reilly, an Aussie bowling great in his day, gave Dell a rave review. 'The bowling honours for the day went to Tony Dell. The giant-sized Queensland left-hander was called upon to do so much work on his baptismal day that I feel doubtful whether he will turn up for the second day's play. I thought he might have considered that one day of this was enough for him. Dell produced a magnificently sustained effort of enthusiastic swing bowling. It was an extremely plucky effort.' Dell's memory of that first day is hazy.

And Bring the Darkness Home

It was late in the afternoon of the second day that the fireworks began. When the Australian tail-end batsman Terry Jenner was hit on the head by a delivery from fast bowler John Snow, the umpire Lou Rowan warned Snow for the 'persistent bowling of fast, short-pitched balls at the batsman'. Snow, who had been warned twice before in the series about bowling too many bouncers, reacted angrily. His captain Illingworth was also furious. Rowan, an Australian, was already unpopular with the England players. In the entire series, during which Rowan umpired all but one match, England received not a single lbw decision.

Now Illingworth went to war on Snow's behalf. He argued Jenner had been to blame, something Jenner himself later admitted. But the mood had turned. As Snow headed down to his fielding position on the boundary in front of Sydney's notoriously raucous 'Hill', he mockingly conducted the baying crowd as if they were an orchestra.

This is how the *Sydney Morning Herald* saw what happened next: 'The Hill crowd, which was in an ugly mood following a series of earlier incidents including a wild all-in brawl where seven people were arrested, loudly booed Snow. Several spectators began shouting abuse at Snow and then began pelting him with bottles and beer cans. Pandemonium broke loose as cans rained on to the ground from all parts of the Hill.' Amid the booing, Snow had gone over to the boundary fence to make peace with some of the crowd. As he reached over to shake hands, one supporter grabbed him by the shirt and tried to slap him in the face. Snow pulled away but the scuffle was enough for Illingworth. Without a word to the umpires he led his team from the field.

40

Chapter 2

It remains one of the most astounding moments in Ashes history, witnessed by the 30,000 in the ground that day and millions who have seen the grainy black-and-white television footage since. The umpires pointed out to Illingworth that refusing to return to the field would, under the laws of the game, result in him forfeiting the match. England did return, seven minutes after they had left the field, and after the bottles and cans had been removed from the outfield. Illingworth later defended his actions, saying he feared for his players' safety: 'I've seen people hit by bottles and it makes a bloody mess. If we had stayed on the field the bottle-throwing could have gone on indefinitely. By going off, we settled the thing quickly.' His actions, though, sharply divided the critics in England and Australia. The former Australian captain turned commentator Richie Benaud backed Illingworth's decision to walk off but lambasted his behaviour towards the umpire. It was, Benaud said, 'not like that of an England captain but more like the prima donna of a South American football team'.

In his newspaper column, O'Reilly said the scenes 'recalled the nerve-tingling memories of the Bodyline days', invoking the spectre of the Ashes of 1932/33 when an on-the-field spat about intimidatory bowling escalated into a diplomatic incident between the two nations' governments.

Tony Dell was watching all of this unfold from the pavilion. If he had wanted a debut to remember, he could not have been disappointed. It adds some irony to the sad fact that his memory of the game is all but non-existent.

Jenner was well enough to return to bat the following morning and Australia finished with a first innings lead. When they bowled again, on that Valentine's Day of 1971, Dell would take some small measure of revenge on England's captain for that dismissal of his abilities. Late on in the day he bowled a ball that struck Illingworth a painful blow on the knee. It was only after a rest day of X-rays and ultrasonic treatment that Illingworth was declared fit to carry on.

Dell took the wickets of three England batsmen in their second innings but Australia lost the match by 62 runs and with it the series and the Ashes. What he remembers of his performance is informed largely by the reviewers of the time. His 'opening spell was wide in direction and erratic in length', one correspondent wrote, something Dell put down to first-match nerves, but he settled down to bowl well. Frank Tyson, the former England fast bowler who terrorised Australia in the 1950s, noted in his newspaper column that Dell 'could be a long-term investment'.

This was a time of transition for the Australian team. The series was written off as having been deadly dull, an 'awful summer of cricket that will look better in the record books'. Illingworth and his opposite number Ian Chappell both called for the Ashes to be scrapped as a concept. So intent were the holders on not losing them that, they believed, it rewarded negative play. It seems no one took their suggestion seriously, and the Ashes continue to rouse English and Australian fans.

As that 1970/71 season ended though, Tony Dell had every reason to believe he had finally launched the top-flight cricket career he so desired. Vietnam had delayed it, doubts about his fitness had frustrated it, but now here he was, part of a new generation of young and promising cricketers, the country hoped, about to change Australia's fortunes. Test cricket, he remembers, had not been the step-up in skill and intensity he had expected. He had not found it a struggle. 'The real difference was the pressure and the realisation that more people were watching,' he said at the time.

Australia's domestic competition, the Sheffield Shield, was then perhaps the strongest first-class contest in the world. For Dell playing in Shield cricket had been the real education. But now he was a Test fast bowler. 'He was the right age, he had the right build, he was there with Lillee, he was a good prospect,' remembers Eastwood. 'I was confident I was there for a while,' said Dell.

There was talk of him spending the 1971 English summer as a professional with a County Championship side. Dell demurred. He chose instead to spend those months correcting what some saw as defects in his bowling action. Tom Graveney was among those encouraging him to shorten his run-up, adjust his delivery stride and change his foot position at the moment of release.

There were plenty of reasons to be hopeful by the time the Australian summer of 1971/72 came around. It was to bring frustration for Dell. The planned tour of Australia by South Africa was cancelled amid fears of a repeat of the anti-apartheid protests that had greeted the Springboks rugby team months earlier. The protests had become so violent that the premier of Queensland had declared a state of emergency. A hastily assembled Rest of the World cricket team toured Australia instead.

Although Dell was taking wickets in a dismal season for Queensland, something was not quite right. The changes to his bowling action seemed to lessen his impact. He began to doubt what those experienced players had told him about the need to change. 'It was a disaster and the moral of that story is if it ain't broke, don't fix it. Halfway through the next season I was back to my old run-up but the damage was done.'

But Graveney was among those full of praise for Dell's return to form that season as the selectors sat down to pick their squad for the Ashes tour of England in 1972.

But away from cricket, Tony Dell's friends had noticed a change in him, far more significant than anything to do with his bowling action. They had seen it from his first days back in Australia in 1968. In their view, it was a change for the worse. The 'gentle giant' that Greg Delaney remembered from their schooldays had become more aggressive. Never physically violent, Delaney said, but prone to fly off the handle in a way that was unexpected and unfamiliar to those who knew him well. He would have 'flashes of anger and tell someone to go and get well and truly fucked. It was a different sort of anger, the sort I'd never seen from him before.'

Through the fog of decades, Dell was able to see some of what he was like back then: 'I was totally oblivious to what I was doing and what I was saying and eventually I got this reputation of being a bit of a prick.' On the cricket field, that new-found aggression perhaps added some spice to his bowling but off the field it would cause years of problems. And his friends had no doubt what was at the heart of that change. 'He came back from Vietnam carrying a lot of baggage with him,' says his schoolfriend Bruce Tanner. There was that aggression. 'He was more shy, more reticent in talking to people unless he knew them.'

Chapter 2

They all saw it, but no one confronted it. In fairness, the concept of challenging a Vietnam veteran about their moods and behaviour, what they had seen and heard, the horrors of war and the invisible scars, was one few were willing to take on at that time.

The years that followed were a story of pain and suffering for Tony Dell and those around him. That story rings bells for those who have seen combat and the people who love them. Many never got to understand it in their lifetimes. It would take decades for Tony Dell to.

It took his memories and, he believes, his cricket career as well. The call for the Ashes in England in 1972 never came and within four years of that Test match debut, and all those hopes and expectations, he had walked away from cricket for good. One more unlikely casualty of the ghosts of the Vietnam War.

3

TONY DELL is unique in being the only Test cricketer to serve in combat in Vietnam. What makes his double service for Australia even more unusual is that, at the time of both, Tony Dell was British. For the first 14 years of his life, home was the battered landscape of post-war Britain. When he was picked to make his debut for Australia in 1971, the country's Department of Immigration and Multicultural and Indigenous Affairs issued a publicity photo of Dell with the caption: 'Migrants in sport in Australia – British born cricketer plays in Test against England'.

The world could be forgiven for missing Anthony Dell's entry into the world on 6 August 1945. It was understandably more preoccupied with the dropping of an atomic bomb on Hiroshima that day. It signalled the beginning of the end of one war for the world – when America launched into another two decades later, it would fully engage Tony Dell.

No one could have predicted that inside the Dell family home. Born in a nursing home in the clifftop town of Barton-on-Sea in Hampshire, young Tony's first home was a small prefab house in the tiny seaside community of Highcliffe.

Chapter 3

What had once been a popular resort destination, all scenic views and a mild, dry climate considered good for the mind and body by the Victorian English, had by then faded. Highcliffe in the 1940s was notable only for its castle and the presence of an eccentric nudist called Gerald Gardner, a tattooed ex-civil servant who founded the modern pagan witchcraft known as 'Wicca'. Today there is a blue plaque on the former home of the man known as the 'King of the Witches' to commemorate his colourful stay there.

Young Dell's memories are more earthly. The thin edge of the street sign for Upper Gordon Road was too tempting for an adventurous four-year-old. The tightrope walk led to the inevitable fall, catching a rusty bolt on the way down. The gash on his left knee needed what he remembered for years as the first stitches of his life.

Highcliffe was idyllic for a child. The long climb down to its beach, looking out across the Solent to the Isle of Wight, and learning to swim in the sea. Family photos tell the story of the odd snowy winter but far more of Tony and his three siblings sunning themselves on the beach or in the back garden.

Dell saw little of his father for the first decade of his life. Alfred Herbert 'Ross' Dell was a rugby player good enough to represent the Royal Navy in its annual match against the Army at Twickenham in 1947. Having left the navy, he took a job with Hoover and, in his son's recollection, spent most of his time working to improve his lot and get rid of his Cockney accent. 'He never ever discussed his war so I know nothing,' says his son. Only once, Dell remembers, did he meet his paternal grandfather, in a dingy flat in London with the old man's second wife. 'They had shipped Dad off to the navy when he was 15 so I guess there wasn't much love there.'

It was Dell's mother Barbara who played the major role in the early lives of her four children. A girl from rural Dorset, like many young women, she did her bit in the war effort working in the munitions factories. She returned to country life and a passion for living off the land. 'My mum did an amazing job bringing up four kids virtually by herself. I just remember her as being the ultimate earth mother who grew most of her own vegetables and raspberries and strawberries.' When her mother would come to visit, Dell stole two shillings from his grandmother's purse. He spent them at the sweet shop with his best friend Billy Bates. 'Two shillings bought a lot of lollies in those days.'

Billy Bates was also there when Dell set fire to an area of scrubland – 'Jesus, that was a big blaze.' They would also pelt the house of a curmudgeonly old major with rocks on the way to the beach. Dell would also be dispatched by his mother to the Cat and Fiddle pub to buy cigarettes for her from the off-licence window. 'There was no such thing as underage in those days.' Every child on the street would gather at the house of the first family to buy a television – the after-school shows became a routine. Remarkably, at the age of six, he was packed off alone on the train to visit his aunt in Leicester, some 160 miles away. 'I must have asked a hundred times, "Is this my stop?"'

Barely a mile from the family's home in Highcliffe was one of England's greatest natural treasures. The New Forest, 200 square miles of woodland, heath and pasture, was then and remains now a home to an abundance of rare wildlife. To a young boy it meant freedom and open space, fields of bluebells and daffodils, rambling and adventuring to fill the summer holidays. It was also the illegal source of the family Christmas tree every year. If the picture is an idyllic one, post-war English life was hard. Rationing continued for nine years after the end of the war. Breakfasts of 'bread and dripping', the leftover fat from the Sunday roast, were the norm for the Dells and a generation of British children.

It was at primary school in Hampshire that, aged six, Tony Dell first played cricket. Twenty years later, the county of his birth would come calling with an approach to sign the then newly minted Australian international. Their interest makes sense: in those days of restrictions on overseas players, they could have registered him as an Englishman.

In the mid-1950s, the Dell family departed Hampshire for Hemel Hempstead in Hertfordshire, rapidly expanding as one of the new towns designated after the war to take some of those displaced by the Blitz of London. Like much in the town, Dell's school was brand new and cricket and football dominated daily life. An attempt at learning the violin was short-lived. For a tall and awkward boy, the memory sticks of being barracked by the headmaster for being ungainly on the football pitch. As a cricketer, his first action came as a wicketkeeper and batsman. It was only playing regularly up against the wall around the family home that he learned to bowl. Like millions of children around the cricket-playing world, games would go on into the twilight.

It was a time when space seemed endless, there were few other distractions, and little traffic on the roads that he played on with the Greenaway boys and the Binders. Robin Binder,

Dell remembered, had the same tangled bowling action as Max Walker.

It was Francis Greenaway who once fished Dell's brother Chris from the water and weeds of the Grand Union Canal. The whole neighbourhood was a playground with the hazard of the lane that became known as 'Bombers Alley'. A colony of rooks had taken up residence in the giant trees that lined the road and overlapped in the middle. The deafening noise was one thing. Dodging the bombardment of droppings was another. The birds' agitation was perhaps explained by the local schoolboy pastime of trying to shoot them out of the tree with a bow and arrow.

The young Dell had a passion for collecting birds' eggs, carefully kept on a bed of sawdust in shallow boxes, duplicates swapped with the like-minded at school. As in Hampshire, nature played its part in family life as his mother was breeding Siamese cats. Spaniels, rabbits, guinea pigs, hamsters, birds and tropical fish all kept on coming and going. In the fields surrounding the newly built housing estate, mushrooms and blackberries were collected up and taken home.

It was in Hemel Hempstead that the first television set arrived in the Dell household. It meant the first notable cricket to appear on Tony Dell's horizon as a child was the Ashes series in England in 1956. It was a summer of men who would become legends of the game: Cowdrey and May, Laker and Lock for England; Harvey and Benaud, Lindwall and Miller for Australia. Like any good young English cricket fan that summer, Dell was glued to the BBC's coverage. 'Us Poms thrashed Australia,' he remembered. Jim Laker took 46 wickets in the series and rewrote cricket's record books by taking 19 wickets at Old Trafford, a feat which has still never been equalled in first-class, let alone Test, cricket. 'Who would have thought that six years later I'd be rubbing shoulders with some of those fellows and playing with and against them in Brisbane?'

Before that, the Dell family was on the move again, this time to Cardiff. A promotion put Ross Dell in charge of Hoover's operations in South Wales. 'He was very dedicated. It was as if he had something to prove.' For his son, it meant life-changing developments: 'In Cardiff I wore long pants to school, became a Boy Scout, first played rugby, became a good left-hand bowler and kissed my first couple of girls.'

The summer of 1958 was as memorable as those Ashes of 1956 for Dell. When Cardiff hosted the Commonwealth Games, dutiful Boy Scouts were put to work. Dell acted as a messenger for news reporters covering the games. It was a sporting education for a young boy. He spent most of his time at the boxing and wrestling but occasionally would tear himself away. Of the stars he saw in action in that damp and miserable summer, it is the Australians who now stick in his mind: the great middle-distance runner Herb Elliott and, in the pool, the dazzling teenage 'Konrads Kids' John and Ilsa, Murray Rose and Dawn Fraser. Swimming became a new passion, for good and bad. In the pool he competed in the Welsh National Championships. Outside of the pool, he suffered a serious knee injury while chasing someone around the side.

Ten days in hospital aged 13 was a lonely experience with just one visit from his parents. Only a crush on a nurse and an introduction to Toblerone kept his spirits up. Weeks in plaster followed before he could rejoin his friends Jimmy and Paul for cricket on the flat bottom of the old reservoir. It was in Cardiff that Dell experienced his first international rugby match, Wales against England at Cardiff Arms Park. 'I stood for about three hours in the rain and cold. I really don't know if I enjoyed it or not.' What was more enjoyable were his visits to Glamorgan's cricket ground, at the time right next to the Arms Park, for the visits of the invincible Surrey team of May, Laker and Lock.

But 1958 also brought sporting tragedy. The vibrant and successful young Manchester United football team, the 'Babes' shaped by their manager Matt Busby, were returning from a European Cup tie in Belgrade that February when their plane crashed in the snow. The disaster in Munich cost the lives of eight players among the 23 people to die. Some of the brightest prospects of English football were lost and, especially to young fans like Dell who had fallen in love with the Babes, it was a time of grief and confusion. United's rise from the ashes of that disaster and the club's future fortunes would come to inspire Dell many years later.

In 1958 though, the sport was coming thick and fast for teenage boys. In June, football's World Cup in Sweden saw Wales take part for the first time. It also saw the arrival on the world stage of a 17-year-old called Pelé.

The English winter of 1958 saw another Ashes battle loom. The team that set off for Australia was labelled the strongest ever to leave England. Captain May had the spin of Laker and Lock, the pace of Fred Trueman, Frank Tyson and Brian Statham, and the batting strength of Colin Cowdrey, Tom Graveney and Ted Dexter. England had won three Ashes series in a row. They returned home in February 1959 having lost four-nil in what was regarded as one of the greatest upsets in Ashes history. The victorious Australians included men who Dell would come to know, including Peter Burge, Wally Grout, Ken Mackay and, most significantly of all, Ray Lindwall.

In gloomy Cardiff, it can hardly have occurred to that young Boy Scout that Aussie sports stardom lay in his own future.

The life-changing news came out of the blue. 'Dad sat us all down and said how would you like to go to Australia to live? This young boy who had been put into the Royal Navy with very little education was now being asked to open up a branch for Hoover in Queensland.'

It wasn't a difficult decision. While Britain was enjoying something of an economic golden age, the country was falling behind the rest of Europe and the world, its time as a global superpower over. Prime Minister Harold Macmillan told Britons, 'Most of our people have never had it so good.' Many were enjoying the fruits of the boom, taking holidays and maybe even buying a new Mini, launched in August 1959 at a price of £500. A surge of immigration into Britain from the Caribbean and Indian subcontinent spoke of a country offering economic hope. But many saw a grey and tattered place still pockmarked by post-war austerity. The fog that enveloped the country in early 1959, the worst since the Great Smog of 1952, was emblematic of how many felt. Only the travel agents and chemists did well: holidays and smog masks sold out. This was not the exciting Britain of the Swinging Sixties. The lure of the sunshine and beach lifestyle of Australia, sweltering in a heatwave at the time, was irresistible.

Ross Dell made the journey by air so, in September 1959, a neatly handwritten ship's manifest for the SS *Orcades* recorded mother and four children setting sail from Tilbury in London's East End, first-class and bound for Australia. The journey took them through the Mediterranean, stopping to visit the ruins at Pompeii, through the Suez Canal and the Red Sea, experiencing the bustling markets of the Middle East, Sri Lanka and the seasickness of the Indian Ocean. On crossing the equator, the children were treated to the traditional ritual of being dunked in the ship's pool by King Neptune. The younger siblings passed the month-long sailing by causing havoc in the off-limits parts of the ship while Tony Dell was crowned ship's table tennis champion. Finally, after sailing halfway around Australia, they drew into Sydney Harbour, the first sight of that coat-hanger bridge, the symbol of welcome for millions making a new life Down Under. The Dells, fully vaccinated according to the immigration arrivals record, were about to embark on their own new adventure.

They joined one of the greatest migration stories in history. Since the war, some 1.5 million had arrived in Australia, half of those from Britain. As the 1960s dawned, more than 130,000 new Australians were arriving every year. By the time the Dells landed, Australia's population had just topped ten million.

Many of those arrivals had taken advantage of the Australian government's Assisted Passage Migration Scheme, the 'populate or perish' policy to supply workers for the booming industrial sector in the country. They were lured with the promise of affordable housing, good jobs, a new and forward-looking country – plus a fare for the journey of just £10. From the UK alone, a million 'Ten Pound Poms' took up the offer between 1945 and 1973. Another campaign to 'Bring out a Briton' kept the flow of migrants coming from the old country, the scheme marking the end of Australia's preferential treatment for arrivals from Britain. The assisted migrants were expected to stay in Australia for two years. Those who chose to return home during that time had to refund the real cost of the journey, usually a prohibitive sum ten times that of the original £10. It is estimated a quarter of the arrivals did return to the UK within those two years, although half of those – 'the Boomerang Poms' – changed their minds again and returned Down Under.

The Poms were not the only new arrivals swelling the Australian population. There were schemes for Italian, Dutch, Greek, German and Turkish arrivals. Residents of Ireland and other British colonies were also encouraged to make the journey. It contributed to a major shift in the diversity of Australian cities. In the early 1960s, it was estimated that nine out of every ten people living in the seaside city of Woollongong, south of Sydney, were migrants, made up of 30 nationalities. Melbourne, a city renowned to this day for its melting pot make-up, saw a surge of new arrivals after the war, mainly Europeans from Greece, Italy and Yugoslavia and those from Lebanon, Cyprus and Turkey. Where the Dells called home in Brisbane, this mix of cultures and backgrounds was also causing a buzz of fascination. Newsreel footage of a cricket match at the Gabba shows two young men, ignoring the strange goings-on out in the middle, deep in their newspapers: the *Maltese Herald* and *La Fiamma*. 'Who wants to know about square leg and Bodyline when the sun's out?' asked the newscaster.

The new arrivals were offered free English lessons if they needed but the shift in demographics went both ways. On the streets of Australian cities, new cafes, delis and restaurants were springing up, offering exotic new tastes. The trend for eating out was growing as Australia was becoming more cosmopolitan.

The attraction for the migrants was obvious: jobs, a good climate and space in which to bring up a family. Seven out of ten Australian homes at the time were owner-occupied and 90,000 new homes were going up every year. The prospect of a home to call their own, with a garden and a standard of living better than where they had left, was too good to refuse. If the dream was to sour for some, the promised homes and jobs not what they were led to expect, for millions Australia proved to be a promised land.

Brisbane, the 'city in the sun', offered quite the contrast to life in a drab Britain. With its palm trees and humid subtropical climate of long, hot, wet summers and dry, warm winters, in the words of those promoting the city as a future home, it was a place 'of dignified but not pretentious buildings, of sunshine and beauty'. The city had been trying to rid itself of a post-war image of being nothing but a big country town. The Dells arrived during a time of a major effort at urban renewal of the central business district and the suburbs, an attempt to put Brisbane on a par with Australia's powerhouse cities. Oil had been discovered in Queensland and refinery construction in Brisbane played a part in a booming economy. Infrastructure problems held up some of the efforts but Brisbane was undoubtedly growing. To many its very appeal was as a leisurely, calm suburban centre, its mood set by the winding river and the ubiquitous poinsettia flowers.

If Brisbane felt different, just down the coast was an attraction that would have felt like it was from another world to new Pommie arrivals. The Gold Coast was a place where it was 'always summer, where the sun and the sand are golden', according to the brochure.

Chapter 3

In Surfers Paradise 'a man can wear a swimming costume and carry a briefcase and no one will even notice'. Even the meter maids were wearing bikinis on the Gold Coast. The shift in the cultural norms as Australia boomed was happening a little too quickly for some. On one weekend on Sydney's Bondi Beach, 75 women were told to leave by lifeguards because their swimming costumes did not meet stiff regulations. The 'bikini wars', happily encouraged by enterprising newspapers, saw 25-year-old dancer and actress Joan Barry fined £3 (Australia did not adopt the dollar until 1966) in court for wearing a swimsuit that was 'at least five inches below the navel'. The offending swimsuit had been confiscated and placed on display at the local police station. One council alderman suggested that women wearing bikinis could parade before members of the council so they could judge their appropriateness before they took the beach. Before that solution went any further, the council simply changed the rules and the bikini war had been won.

What a new world this was for Tony Dell. Back on the Gold Coast, the more pure of heart could take buses up into mountains rich with tropical delights of bananas, pineapples and mangoes.

The transition to this beach and sunshine lifestyle was undoubtedly easier for the children who arrived as migrants. In a new, young country where every day felt like a holiday, anything seemed possible. If some of their parents felt ill at ease thousands of miles from their old homes, the children they brought with them became Aussies in a heartbeat.

'For me it was a brand-new world where the pathway in front of me was so very different to the one that might have existed in England,' said Dell.

They arrived into the warmth of a Queensland spring. The adjustment to the heat, Dell said, was the hardest thing to get used to; all that sunning themselves on the beach in Highcliffe had at least given them a grounding. The family's first home in Australia was in the Brisbane suburb of Newmarket, a place once known as 'Three Mile Scrub' for its landscape and distance from the centre of the city. Like much of Brisbane, the housing stock was what were known as Queenslander-style houses, timber-built with high ceilings and big verandahs, often the houses lifted up on stilts to elevate them into the cooling breeze.

More practically, living in Newmarket meant a complex journey by tram through central Brisbane for the young Dell to reach the place that would define much of the rest of his life: Brisbane's prestigious Church of England Grammar School, known as Churchie. Some of the friendships from those early days at school were to be become lifelong. But at first, Dell found he was something of an enigma with his classmates. He was a 'Pom' after all. When they found out the tall Pom could bowl a bit, life became immeasurably easier. 'A new school with a new way of life, the opportunities afforded by a sport I was good at,' Dell said later, buzzing at the possibilities Australia offered.

After the family's first tropical Christmas, they moved to the suburb of Coorparoo. He became friends with Greg Delaney on the school bus. They lived a few hundred yards apart and would get off the bus at the same stop. 'Everyone noticed he was tall. We were all 6ft but he was 6ft 4, 6ft 5, and that made all the difference,' remembers Delaney. The backyard cricket matches infuriated Delaney's father, the pitches gouging great chunks out of his prized lawns. Dell's own father was a little more forgiving. Peter Buchanan, who lived next door on Cavendish Road, remembers a garden 'manicured to provide a batting strip, although the rectangular dimensions necessitated a diagonal layout of the strip to accommodate something close to 22 yards'. Wherever they played, facing the giant left-armer was a challenge.

'We all used a cricket ball but we wouldn't let him bowl at us with a cricket ball so he had to use a tennis ball,' Delaney said. Even with a tennis ball, Dell once shattered the fruit box they used for stumps. 'That tennis ball was just a blur to me, I'd just swipe at it. I wouldn't be here today if we'd let him bowl with a proper ball.' It did not go unnoticed at Churchie.

As one of the school's cricket captains, Gary Bird recalls it took a while for Dell's pace to arrive. When the first XI coach unexpectedly left him out of the annual match against the Sydney Church of England Grammar School, something changed. 'I believe this is where his career began and he became an express fast bowler. His run-up speeded up as did his delivery,' said Bird. Facing Dell in the nets, he said, 'was quite harrowing'. The opening bowling partnership of Dell and future Australian rugby international David Taylor was also a pretty harrowing experience for most of the school's opponents. In one match, Dell took five wickets for two runs, Taylor four for six, the opposition dismissed for a total of eight.

In those school days, Ross Johnston was often the wicketkeeper, a foot shorter in height but, in his words a shit-stirrer who would give the fast bowler plenty of abuse to fire him up. But Johnston also says he saw a trait in Dell as a teenager that he believes persisted in future relationships. Johnston says Dell held an enduring grudge against the player selected ahead of him for that Sydney game and the coach who made the selection. It is an 'intolerance' he says has never gone away. 'Delly is unbelievably caring and if I needed someone to help with something, I would not hesitate to call him and I'd know he'd be there. But he has got this mental block about some people.'

Friends from the time remember Dell as affable and easy-going. It was his cricketing mates at Churchie who introduced Dell to the Easts club. While still at school, he played his first grade match against Toombul, alongside Peter Burge and against Wally Grout and Ken Mackay, players he had watched on television in the Ashes just a few years before. One legendary Australian cricketer who took an interest in Dell's progress was Ray Lindwall. Regarded as one of the finest fast bowlers in history, Lindwall had ended his career with Queensland and, during coaching sessions at the Langlands Park home of the Easts, helped Dell develop a more side-on bowling action. 'Ray gave me a number of bowling tips and his coaching has been a tremendous help to me,' Dell told reporters on the eve of his Test debut.

Away from the cricket and rugby fields, Dell's teenage years in Brisbane had one other dominant feature.

Every weekend, as Greg Delaney's parents headed out to the racing, barely had their car disappeared from view than, at the other end of the street, another one appeared, loaded down with revellers and a keg of beer. The party would run on long into the night. Delaney still has a faded home movie of the night when a taxi driver, having dropped off one guest for a night of drinking, ended up staying and joining the party himself. The young Tony Dell is unmistakable in those flickering images, taller than everyone else, at the centre of the party.

When the party was not in the street in Coorparoo, it was down the coast. This presented a problem for potless teenagers: finding the money for petrol. The solution presented itself with an elaborate night-time scheme of 'milking' local cars of their fuel and storing it in a can in the bushes. This secured, they went in search of a car. Dell once persuaded his dad to let him borrow the family car, on the understanding it was for a short drive to Mount Gravatt. When the car refused to start at dawn the following morning, 60 miles away in Southport, after a party at the home of his friend Malcolm Nutt, desperate measures were required. Nutt pushed Dell in his own car, bumper-to-bumper, all the way home.

Peter Buchanan remembers another occasion when Dell took advantage of his dad being away to borrow his smart new Rover. While trying to return it quietly to its parking spot, he neglected to stop and drove into the side of the house. 'Ross was a generous fellow overall but could be impassioned if aroused,' said Buchanan. 'I think we all heard the verbals resonating next door later in the day when he got home.'

When the time came to leave school life behind and head out into the workplace, Dell had planned out a career course. 'I left school wanting to become an architect,' he remembered. He spent some time with the well-known Brisbane architect Donald Spencer while studying at Queensland University of Technology but a downturn in Spencer's work led to a series of part-time jobs, as greenskeeper's assistant at bowls clubs and at a petrol station. When he called in sick for a Saturday shift to attend a

Queensland cricket training camp he thought no one would be any the wiser. 'My photograph was in the paper running out of the surf and I got sacked.'

By then he had been taking evening classes in advertising run by John Garnsey, the 'gentle lion' of the city's business world. It led to a job as a media and production manager. 'I loved it and could never work out why I wanted to be an architect,' Dell said. His boss at the agency, Johnny Green, was a fellow Churchie old boy and a friend of Dell's dad. He would come to revel in his young employee's future cricket career.

For a young man, newly settled in a new country, life seemed to be working out well. He had a girlfriend called Shirley, a relationship that felt serious, and his sporting life was on the up. 'I was playing good cricket, getting plenty of wickets and I was the bowler most batsmen in Brisbane didn't want to face,' he remembered.

Then his birth date came out of the National Service hat, so 6 August, Hiroshima and all, had landed Tony Dell in the army. 'Work was good, cricket was good and then I got called up. Jesus, that was the last thing I wanted. A great advertising and cricket career were about to be nipped in the bud and, on top of that, I was going to be away from my girlfriend for two years.'

4

TONY DELL wasn't at home on the Friday evening that Greg Delaney called round to his flat in East Brisbane. Delaney was there to share a few beers with Dell's flatmate Phil McWatters. As the evening wore on, Delaney remembers, they started looking for something in the flat. During the search they came across Dell's battalion book, the official history of the deployment in Vietnam, the two black-bound volumes issued to the soldiers when they returned home. As the pair flicked through its pages, they stopped at a photograph: 'It was just a back country road in Vietnam and a row of bodies.' They thought they could also make out Dell in the photo, rifle over his shoulder, as soldiers apparently searched the bodies. Of the dead, he remembered, a lot of them were only young. As the pair stared at that photo, Dell came home.

'He just went off his brain. "Don't fucking touch that ever again. Don't look at that shit." He went right off.' As his friend ranted and raved, Delaney said: 'I thought to myself, "Shit. This stuff has really affected him." I realised he just didn't want anyone to see it.' What struck Delaney most about that photo is something that he believes would have particularly haunted Dell. 'Probably the age of them got to him. There were also a lot of women amongst them.'

What Delaney remembers of that battalion book decades later is almost completely accurate. Open the book to page 143 and you see the scenes he describes, although actually spread over two photographs. In the first Dell, his head cropped out of the photo but unmistakable to his friends, stands with his hands on his hips as possessions collected from the dead enemy are searched. Piled up on the ground are a stack of rifles, ammunition and what appear to be mines, alongside a bundle of rags. In the second photo, three bodies lie on a grassy track. It is hard to make out their age or gender but they are frozen in the macabre pose of instantaneous death. The caption accompanying the photos reads: 'A successful ambush'.

Delaney was shocked by his old friend's reaction. It was the moment he saw that the gentle giant of their schooldays had changed. 'He was never a violent person. I can guarantee he would never strike anyone, woman or bloke, but he would fly off the handle and he could be verbally violent.' He never mentioned the incident again. It was obvious to those who knew Dell well that Vietnam had fundamentally altered him. They were old friends, they would adjust, they would accept Dell as he was now but it was alarming all the same. 'It turned an otherwise passive guy into a bit of an angry man.'

This would be the story of the next 40 years of Tony Dell's life. From his return in 1968 onwards, things started to fall apart: dark moods and the anti-social behaviour became familiar companions. Whether he ever questioned why, whether he ever looked into the abyss, isn't clear. There's no doubt he took the path chosen by so many who have been damaged on a deep psychological level. He shut it away, buried it deep in his subconscious, allowing it to ferment just enough to bubble to the surface every now and then and upset the flow of a normal life.

All of it starts with his transition from soldier to civilian. Everyone who was around Tony Dell when he came home from Vietnam remembers how he described it: 'One day I was in the jungle shooting at people, two days later I was walking down Queen Street in Brisbane and looking to get back to work.' Years later it remained one of the few things that was clear in his memory. 'A quick visit to a barracks somewhere, collect your final military pay, a handshake and goodbye. That was it.'

He had come home to an Australia roiling with anti-Vietnam protests and the hippy vibe of the Summer of Love. 'The major shock was the mini-skirts. I couldn't believe them. Everything was different. We were big, bronzed, battle-weary ANZACs in jungle-greens coming into a world of long-haired, colourful protesting wankers. What a culture shock.' He felt adrift, all the more because his parents had moved away from Brisbane. There was no counselling and no one asked him about his war, least of all his family. He didn't talk about it either. As he would tell reporters later in life: 'The army teaches you to kill but they don't unteach you.' These highly trained killing machines, fresh off the battlefield and sizzling with the emotional energy of combat, were plonked right back into the nine-to-five. Fighting in Vietnam, the first war of the jet age, meant they were whisked back to their normal lives with little or no time to adjust or decompress.

He wasn't the only one telling a version of that transition story.

Over the years the families of countless Vietnam veterans have heard and retold it too. Even a theatre review in the late 90s could start with the story of a Vietnam veteran, heard on the radio, describing how a day that started with a routine patrol in the jungle led to an ambush and firefight, being airlifted out by chopper and put on a Qantas jumbo jet home. It wasn't Queen Street in Brisbane but it may as well have been: 'Twenty-four hours later he was standing in George Street, Sydney.' For the next six months, so the story went, he would walk around Sydney, watching the people passing by and thinking 'I could kill you, and you, and you.'

The signs of a restive mind were evident to everyone. Dell's first few months back in Brisbane coincided with the dying days of the city's tram network. One tram line ran directly past that flat on Lisburn Street in East Brisbane. More than once, friends from the time remember, the former soldier would leap from his bed, startled by the early morning screeching of tram brakes, and apparently scrambling to find an imaginary rifle. 'I don't remember it,' Dell would say years later, 'but people told me about it often enough so I guess it did happen. It would make sense. It is one of those fight or flight things. That was what was ingrained into us for two years.'

There were other incidents which showed friends that things were different. Bruce Tanner remembers jokingly grabbing his old schoolfriend from behind during a rugby match. 'I thought he was going to kill me,' says Tanner. 'He was so incensed.' It would never have happened like that before Vietnam.

For Tony Dell much of that period of his life had become a blur in later years. 'He has shut a lot of that out of his mind,' says Greg Delaney.

Even the memory of his exploits on the cricket field during that time is a lost land to Tony Dell. Fortunately, it is a sport defined in part by statistics so the black and white of the numbers at least give us the outline of his career. He had taken 20 wickets in eight matches in that debut season of 1970/71, enough to earn him his first call-up to the national team, but Queensland didn't win a match. The following season they won just one and, amid the tinkering with his bowling run-up, Dell turned in fewer eye-catching performances. It was in the following season that he found his cricketing feet again.

It didn't start well. An injury to his Achilles tendon and strong performances from Queensland's other opening bowlers kept Dell out of the first three matches in the domestic Sheffield Shield competition. He returned for the match against the reigning Shield holders Western Australia in Brisbane in November 1972. In their second innings, Western Australia were bowled out for just 54, a resurgent Dell taking 6-17, figures that would remain his best-ever in first-class cricket.

The next match, against the Pakistani tourists, was unremarkable except for a last-wicket stand of 23 with Trevor Hohns and a whack on the knee from Sarfraz Nawaz during it. But in the next, he again took six wickets and remained a potent force for the rest of the season. 'The 27-year-old Dell has made a splendid comeback to first-class cricket after being written off last season,' wrote Phil Wilkins in the *Sydney Morning Herald*. It was not enough to force a way back into the minds of the Australian selectors though. The bowling attack that flew off to the West Indies at the end of that season looked much like that which had toured England the previous winter. Dell would have to wait for his chance for another crack at the highest level.

Just before that Christmas of 1972, if he had been reading his newspapers, Tony Dell might have seen a story from Saigon about a group of Australian soldiers buying souvenirs and preparing for the journey back to Sydney. Their return home would mark the end of the Australian military involvement in Vietnam. The last soldiers had finished training local South Vietnamese militia and celebrated in traditional style, according to a newspaper report: 'They were booked into one of Saigon's biggest hotels and they carried on their singing, drinking and celebrating well into the night.'

There was little fanfare in Australia about their return home. Strangely, it was the *New York Times* that offered a short and poignant report of their landing back at an air force base near Sydney. The 66 men had received a 'muted welcome', the newspaper reported, with just a few dozen relatives present. 'It seems clear that Australian attitudes towards involvement in Vietnam have changed,' the report went on. The men who returned today were non-committal. An enlisted man, asked whether he thought the commitment had been worthwhile, replied: 'What I think doesn't really matter, does it?'

They returned to a country in a time of major economic and social change. The election of 1972 had seen the end of a near quarter of a century of liberal coalition government and the return of the Labour Party to power. It was in his first few days as prime minister that Gough Whitlam ended Australia's Vietnam War and abolished conscription.

Tony Dell's life was a long way removed from Vietnam by the time the war ended for his compatriots. Despite the disappointment of missing out on the West Indies tour, on and off the cricket field, he appeared outwardly to be a man who had everything going for him – a successful sportsman who had become a director of one of the largest advertising agencies in Brisbane. Inwardly, things were very different. Ever since returning from Vietnam, Tony Dell had had trouble sleeping. When he did sleep, he suffered nightmares. Haunted by visions of dead and disfigured bodies, jolted by flashbacks of enemy fire whistling overhead. Years later he would talk of night sweats and teeth grinding, a fear of crowds. He was introverted and anxious. For decades, he said, if he went into an unfamiliar room, he would always sit facing out, his back to the wall.

There was also that extra aggression on the cricket field, a change in playing personality that so many friends and colleagues had noticed. 'I don't think it was something I thought about consciously, it just happened. That was probably the first sign that things were not as they had been. But I didn't notice that I was any different.' Brothers Greg and Ian Chappell, his captains at state and international level, were unaware that he had even been in Vietnam. 'They probably thought I'd just been born an aggressive prick.'

In hindsight it became obvious to him what was going on in his mind. Back then, like most of society, he admits he was oblivious, and cricket, like work, was a useful distraction.

By the time of the Australian winter of 1973, Queensland's cricket fans could have been forgiven for abandoning all hope.

The state had endured a dismal decade and the authorities decided it called for drastic action. Greg Chappell was the 24-year-old vice-captain of South Australia, playing under the leadership of his brother Ian. Queensland's offer of the captaincy and, according to the newspaper reports of the time, a contract worth $50,000 over three years, was enough to tempt him to move north. Chappell was by then already regarded as one of the finest batsmen in the world. Of his century against England at Lord's in 1972, Richie Benaud wrote: 'I thought it close to the most flawless innings I had ever seen.' On the tour of the Caribbean the following year, he achieved the remarkable feat of scoring 1,000 runs. The Australian team was enjoying a rebirth and Greg Chappell was its leading light. He also had his own ambitions to one day follow his brother as captain of Australia and saying yes to Queensland was a step in that direction. He name-checked Tony Dell as part of the 'good attack' he would lead. The pair would become lifelong friends.

The sort of money on offer to a young superstar like Greg Chappell might not seem outlandish now but it was significant at a time when cricket was no place even to make a living. Players were paid $40 for a Sheffield Shield appearance – as one newspaper columnist put it, 'Queensland have never had a silver spoon to chew on – only the wooden spoon' – and that relative sporting poverty prompted an enterprising solution from one of the state's former players. Lew Cooper had been a Queensland wicketkeeper before taking over the running of the Cricketers Club bar at the Gabba ground. After watching the home side suffer another thrashing in 1972, he proposed an incentive scheme for the team. Any batsman who scored a century would receive $50 with an extra dollar for every run that followed. A bowler who took five wickets in an innings would pick up $25 with another $25 for every extra wicket. Five catches in an innings would win $25 and there would be $20 a head for a win. As word of the scheme spread, local businesses chipped in with donations. The next match was Dell's big comeback against the reigning Shield holders Western Australia.

It did the trick. In that match, Sam Trimble's 127 earned him $77 – every time he hit a boundary after reaching his century, Cooper reported, 'The members were on to me about having to pay up another $4 but it was worth every cent' – and Tony Dell's career-best 6-17 earned him $50. 'Money well spent,' said the keeper of the Cricketers Club bar. Western Australia still went on to retain the Sheffield Shield.

Despite that rare win Queensland had finished rock bottom of the Shield in that season of 1972/73. The following year though, they were transformed. Chappell's captaincy and epic run-scoring – he made more than anyone else in Australia that season and twice as many as any of his new Queensland team-mates – meant they were suddenly a different proposition. The swashbuckling Pakistani batsman Majid Khan – one of only a handful of batsmen to score a century before lunch on the first day of a Test match – added an international flavour to a team that went unbeaten in its first seven matches. Tony Dell was on fire too. Only four bowlers in the country would end the season with more than his 43 wickets.

Against the touring New Zealanders in December at the Gabba, he took six wickets in each innings as Queensland rolled over the Kiwis in two days of a scheduled four-day game. Finishing a match with figures of 12-63 on a Saturday was especially fortuitous. The Australian selectors were due to meet on Monday to pick the Test team to face the shell-shocked New Zealanders. 'Dell was the real star of the match,' raved one report, suggesting that he 'undoubtedly has more to offer as a Test player.'

Dell's return to the international scene was duly confirmed. At 28 years old, once again it seemed his sporting career was back on track. The reaction in the cricketing community was positive; here was a bowler with experience and the capability to unsettle batsmen of international calibre. Another Ashes series was a year away and Tony Dell was back among the cricketing elite. At least that's how it appeared.

The first Test was played at the cavernous Melbourne Cricket Ground, a stadium so vast it once held a crowd of 120,000 for an Australian Rules football final. The match straddled the New Year and proved to be almost as one-sided as the Kiwis' warm-up game against Dell and Queensland. The Aussies piled up a huge first innings total and dismissed the New Zealanders cheaply twice. Tony Dell's only wicket in the match was that of opening batsman Glenn Turner. In truth, he was overshadowed in the first innings by debutant Gary Gilmour, like him a fast left-arm bowler, and by the spinners Kerry O'Keefe and Ashley Mallett in the second innings. As a comeback, apparently in the form of his life, it was an anticlimax and the reviews of Dell's performance were underwhelming. It had been agreed that he, Gilmour and Max Walker would share the two opening bowling spots over the first two Test matches. Consequently, Walker took Dell's place for the second Test in Sydney.

Chapter 4

As Dell watched the action from the pavilion as twelfth man at the Sydney Cricket Ground that early January, he felt unsettled. Five years back from Vietnam, he could sense that something inside of him was beginning to unravel. What those feelings were, what they meant, he couldn't put into words. For a sportsman it was easier to focus on other reasons for the unease.

During that Test, Dell asked for a quiet chat with Neil Harvey. The Aussie batting legend turned selector had twice seen enough potential in Dell to pick him for his country. Now, in January 1974, Dell told Harvey he had had enough.

'Queensland fast bowler Tony Dell has told Australian Test selector Neil Harvey he feels he is washed up as a Test bowler,' read *The Age* in Melbourne. He did not want to be considered for the next Test match nor for a tour to New Zealand the following month. The message was simple: Dell was done with Test cricket. He told the newspaper his groin had troubled him for years and a damaged shoulder meant he could no longer put his back into his bowling. He could play state cricket, he said, but that was that.

Dell got his wish: he was dropped from the squad for the final Test. 'He claims he has become a bowling wreck,' read a newspaper report on the affair. Two Test matches in three years, and Dell's career at the top level was finished.

In old age, he had no recollection of telling selectors or reporters about any excessive physical toll of bowling. There was something else that made no sense to him by then. Within days he was playing for Queensland again and would play all of their remaining games that season. In those four matches he bowled close to 100 eight-ball overs. On top of that, he says, there were the 'hundreds we used to bowl in practice. In those days we didn't have ground bowlers or bowling machines. The only way batsmen got practice was from us. It wasn't uncommon to bowl for two and a half hours. What groin? What shoulder?'

Why then would he have blamed wear and tear on his body for giving up top-level cricket? Back then, he says, physical injuries were a better excuse. In other words, no one talked about mental health, certainly not in the macho world of top-level sport.

There is a tinge of regret today: 'I was Australia's most difficult proposition on greenish wickets at that time. Why else would I have given up the opportunity to bowl on those wickets?'

Having walked away from Test cricket, he appeared content to keep playing for Queensland. The state lost two of their last four games, allowing Victoria to take the Sheffield Shield but securing second place for Queensland. Not a silver spoon, true, but definitely not the wooden one either. There were reasons for the banana-benders, as Queenslanders were known, to be optimistic.

In their final match of that season they had felt the full force of a cricketing tornado which had been churning its way across the country. Jeff Thomson dismissed seven Queensland batsmen in the first innings of a match in Sydney and his New South Wales side won the game comfortably. Thomson, with his mane of hair and catapult-like action, had confirmed his electrifying potential. He had played one Test against Pakistan in December 1972 but a broken bone in his foot had reduced his effectiveness. Now he was back and firing and seemingly enjoying every minute. He was reprimanded for an article in *The Cricketer* magazine in which he described flattening a batsman in a club game: 'The sound of the ball hitting his skull was music to my ears.' By July of 1974 he was also unemployed. He had lost his job as a sales rep because of the amount of time he was taking off to play cricket. It was an occupational hazard for cricketers in those days, and one which would come to bedevil Tony Dell as well.

Having lured Greg Chappell to Brisbane 12 months earlier, Queensland now made a lucrative offer to Thomson. Part of the deal was a job as well and Thommo said yes. The reason why Queensland were on the lookout for a new fast bowler was a bombshell: the state had announced that Tony Dell was not likely to be available for the new season.

Dell's recollections of that decision to quit top-class cricket would become hazy. He told the chairman of selectors Sam Loxton that he was finished with cricket. Loxton told him to tell Greg Chappell – and wished him luck breaking the news. Chappell simply refused to accept the decision. 'Bullshit, I've got Thommo coming next season and I want you to open the bowling with him.' Dell agreed to play on for one more year.

That season, with Thomson now representing Queensland, is one that still sends a chill down the spine of some Englishmen. In the Ashes series of 1974/75, Australia devastated an England team terrorised by the bowling of Thomson and Dennis Lillee. 'Never,' *Wisden* observed, 'have batsmen been so grievously bruised and battered by ferocious, hostile, short-pitched balls.' When he wasn't tormenting England's batsmen for Australia's Test team, Thomson formed an effective partnership with Tony Dell for his new state. 'Thommo was totally fearsome in those days,' said Dell. 'Here I was, opening the bowling with the fastest bowler in the world. Ever.' It was another productive season for Dell, and for Queensland it ended with another second place.

This time Dell was done for good. His first-class career ended at home at the Gabba on 10 March 1975. He took a few wickets in a comfortable win over Victoria, Thomson taking the headlines in his first match back after a shoulder injury sustained while playing tennis. At the age of 29, Tony Dell walked away from senior cricket.

It would take him years to pick through the feelings and emotions and reach the conclusion that he had gone too early. He came to realise that the reasons for giving up had very little to do with cricket.

'I was stunned when he walked away from it,' says his lifelong friend Greg Delaney. 'He could have gone a lot further.'

Greg Chappell was equally surprised. 'I was taken aback when he said he was going to retire. I knew that he could have been an important part of any success we had. But he had a real struggle and it is a shame it wasn't something he was able to talk about because, if he had, things could have turned out very differently.'

Dell wasn't even able to revisit memories of his stunted playing career. They have simply vanished. 'I have bursts. The thrill of playing a Test match with Ian and Greg Chappell, Rod Marsh, Dennis Lillee was out of this world and there's a bit I remember. I remember a few wickets I took but by and large it's a mystery.'

Chappell said: 'There's no doubt he could have played more Tests. The timing would have been perfect.' He ponders a bowling attack of Lillee, Thomson and Dell. 'It would have been a fair handful, a formidable attack certainly in Australia.' One downside, the captain recognised, of having those three in the team: 'It would have put a lot of pressure on our batsmen, because there wouldn't have been many runs from those as a last three.'

Chapter 4

Chappell believes Dell should have pursued the possibility of playing county cricket for his native Hampshire in 1971. The bowlers he compares to Dell, tall and awkward customers like the West Indian Joel Garner and South African Vintcent van der Bijl benefitted, in Chappell's view, from their time playing for Somerset and Middlesex. 'It would have given his bowling another dimension.' He would also have played alongside Barry Richards, the man who did so much to propel him into the selectors' thinking.

Some of cricket's reference books give differing accounts of Dell's reasons for quitting the game. What he obviously told many people back then was that he was unavailable for cricket for work reasons.

As Jeff Thomson had found out to his cost, the amount of time first-class cricketers had to spend away from their day jobs was extensive. It left Tony Dell feeling guilty, and the roots of that guilt were in Vietnam. 'Teamwork in cricket and in war is similar. You're only as strong as the weakest member and I had all these pangs of guilt at leaving my workmates to cover for me while I was off playing cricket. I guess I felt I was the weakest member of my workplace. I never really knew why at the time. My rationale there was, "I'm not there, there's other people doing my job, that's not fair." Back then, your job and job security were much more important than sport, there was no money in sport.'

To assuage his guilt for taking time away from his job, Tony Dell became a workaholic. As his cricket career came to an end, his career with the advertising agency Clemengers in Brisbane was taking off. 'I'd get up at the crack of dawn, go to work and wouldn't come home until late.' But, in 1980, he was fired after 15 years with the firm. 'I'd even given up cricket for them.' He says it was some time before he learned the reasons for his dismissal. 'Here we had the old strength of the platoon thing again. It seems I was rather hard on people not pulling their weight so I had to go. It works in the army but not in business.' Away from the office, he says, he was gaining a reputation as a social misfit. His answer was to avoid ever having to work for a boss again.

The 1980s and a new business partnership brought success and excitement but it came to an end after eight years when he was fired again. 'Again, no real reason given. Was I just rubbing everyone up the wrong way again?' Yet another fresh start came to a juddering halt. Not his personality this time but a global economic crisis.

'The recession we had to have,' was how Australia's treasurer Paul Keating described a crisis that was the worst to hit Australia since the Great Depression. Share prices plunged 40 per cent and interest rates soared. What had started with the global stock market crash of Black Monday in 1987 would end up bringing down financial institutions across Australia. It also crippled the Dell Partnership. 'I lost everything,' he said.

Ross Johnston had played cricket with Dell when they were teenagers. He had regularly been on the end of some barrages of bad language back then. The pair had lost touch after school and had no contact through Dell's Vietnam years. He remembers sneaking out of the office in 1971 to listen to the radio in his Hillman Minx as his old friend made his Test debut. 'I was living in Melbourne and he was in Brisbane and we didn't have anything to do with each other but I was excited that he was playing for Australia.'

Chapter 4

The old friends reconnected just as Dell's life was beginning to unravel. This is what Johnston saw: 'He always thought people had let him down. Most of the time people just couldn't be bothered dealing with his antics. He was very black and white. If someone did something to him he'd never want to talk to them again. He'd cut them out of his life.'

For Dell, the 1990s brought little improvement in his fortunes. 'A forgettable, nightmare decade. How I got through it is a mystery to me.' He admits he lost the will to get up and start again in advertising. It was the darkest period of his life. Debts piled up, letters from the tax authorities went unopened, unknown to him fines steadily accumulating. He moved from rental property to rental property and eventually ended up living in the garage of his mother's home in the town of Caloundra on the Sunshine Coast.

His friends remember visiting him there. Greg Delaney says Dell refused his offers of help, even to get a pair of glasses he needed. Ross Johnston described Dell's state as 'bloody awful'. He said: 'He used to walk around in a dirty old pair of tracksuit pants, shirt hanging out, unshaven. He was just slumped and slovenly.' For those who knew him well, and for Tony Dell himself, he had hit rock bottom.

From there, it would take a series of events to lead Tony Dell to a moment of discovery. It would make sense of the last 40 years of his life and reveal to him just how damaged he was. It would also show him the way to a life of renewed purpose.

It all changed when he was diagnosed with post-traumatic stress disorder.

It was a turning point in his life. All the foggy memories, all the anger, all the intolerance – now it appeared there was an explanation. What had been impossible to get straight in his own mind now seemed to fit together. At the root of it all, he could see, was what he had been exposed to in Vietnam. Even the decision to walk away from top-level cricket now was easier to understand. Those problems with groin and shoulder that he blamed? 'I just didn't want to admit that I had a mental problem. Since I was diagnosed, I've come to the conclusion that I gave cricket away without really knowing why.'

In summary, he had endured '40 years of crap when deep down you think you're normal'. But as well as the businesses, the cars, the houses, Tony Dell lost something else as a result of the chaos. 'I had three kids under the age of nine and my marriage was disintegrating.'

5

WHEN THE teenage Tony Dell and his friends were carrying out those surreptitious 'milking' raids on the car petrol tanks in Coorparoo, there was one target about whom he would later come to feel a little sheepish. Hector Spring had won the Distinguished Flying Cross for his heroics over Europe as a pilot officer with the Royal Australian Air Force in World War Two. He was also destined to become Tony Dell's father-in-law.

If Tony Dell had no idea who Katie Spring was back then, she was to come to be the closest observer of a life unravelling. Through Tony Dell's career highs and personal lows, and throughout his battle with the hidden scars of Vietnam, Katie Dell bore the brunt. The couple's marriage had to weather a storm of troubles from a brooding giant struggling with his past. It caused years of pain and distress and was to end in acrimony and regret.

As a young man, Tony Dell believed his biggest problem with women was forming a relationship at all. He was a shy teenager and his schoolfriend Greg Delaney's recollection of 'plenty of girls hanging around' the budding cricket star appears to have been lost on Dell himself. Before he was deployed to Vietnam he had been dating a young woman called Shirley Lobb. They had been a couple for four years and Delaney remembers taking Shirley to the quayside as Dell sailed off to war. At the very last moment the emotional wave goodbye would have been visible from ship to shore, Delaney mischievously slipped his arm around Shirley's shoulder. 'About two weeks later I got the filthiest letter you've ever seen in your life. "You f---ing dickhead", this and that,' Delaney remembers.

Dell's romance with Shirley survived that joke. For 12 months the couple wrote letters back and forth from Australia to Vietnam. Dell says he was 'besotted, she was the first love of my life'. In the jungle, he carried a small photograph of her in a waterproof plastic bag. While other soldiers used their rest and relaxation leave to head to some of the seedier attractions in the city of Vung Tau, Dell flew a thousand miles to Hong Kong to buy an engagement ring for Shirley. At the end of his tour in Vietnam, Dell's company returned to Australia via Sydney. Shirley was waiting for him at the airport. They spent the evening together and the next day she told him she had met someone else. 'At least she didn't write me a Dear John letter when I was out there,' he says. The news was shattering to the 22-year-old. It would be a while before he ventured on to the romantic scene again.

Dell says he has always had difficulties in relating to partners. He thought of himself as a one-woman man. When team-mates on cricket tours were off chasing women he would find himself at a loss. The one exception to his rule, and a completely innocent one at the time, was to come years later, in Adelaide in February 1973. It was to be a friendship with a young woman that would fundamentally alter the path of his life, but not until some 40 years later.

A few years after he was dumped by Shirley, back home in Brisbane, Dell had begun a relationship with a hairdresser called Teresa Gil. Like him she was a transplant from England and the couple moved in together in a small house near a convent school close to Dell's childhood home in Coorparoo. The relationship with his fellow Pom was to prove problematic though, when Katie came to work at his advertising agency.

At first the pair clicked merely as friends. Dell remembers Katie, like him, as shy and vulnerable. She was also married. Not that that stopped Dell making eyes at her across the office. This mild flirting came to an end when she abruptly left the company. She returned shortly afterwards, by then, to an open-plan office with half partitions, perfect elbow-height for Dell to hang around and chat, and things began to get serious. The shared conversations became lunches together. Dell remembers that the first kiss came before Katie, her marriage already on the ropes, had started divorce proceedings. Her marriage was not the only complication. Dell was still living with Teresa. 'They both knew about each other and for a while things got rather ugly. I was given an ultimatum by both of them.'

At first, Dell remembers, he decided to stay with Teresa. When she moved to Sydney shortly afterwards, he resumed his relationship with Katie. It proved useful fitness training: he would run to her place in the evening, spend the night and run home again in the morning, pinching a newspaper and bottle of milk for breakfast from a front yard along the way. The couple eventually found their own flat together. By this time, Dell says, he had fallen in love with Katie. The blossoming romance meant reacquainting himself with the man whose petrol he had pilfered a decade earlier, Katie's father Hector and her mother Minnie. During weekend visits to the family home in Southport on the Gold Coast, Dell stayed in the Pacific Hotel down the road to maintain the impression of propriety. In return, Katie had the pleasure of meeting Dell's circle of friends, an experience, he joked, that changed her life forever. One weekday lunchtime in 1975, with just Greg Delaney and his wife for company, they paid a visit to a lawyer's office in Brisbane and got married. They went back to work and spent the afternoon telling colleagues and inviting them to a party that night, before remembering they had better tell their parents as well.

Marriage came at precisely the moment Dell was giving away his first-class cricket career. Thirty years old with a burgeoning business life and seven years removed from his time in Vietnam, few knew a time bomb was ticking.

The first five years of married life passed in a blur. Business was booming, houses were bought, club cricket played and there were trips to Hong Kong and Singapore. Life was a whirl of lunches, parties, weekends at the coast, club cricket and gambling nights. It was never dull. Some of the happiest times were spent on the beach at Southport, close to Katie's parents. The couple lived, worked and played together seven days a week, a round-the-clock proximity that seemed to pose no problems at the time. In fact, Dell says, it seemed to be the spark for his wife's creative skills: 'I think a happy personal and home life is an important aspect for creative writing and I reckon that Katie really started to fire from then on.'

Chapter 5

That professional admiration for his wife as a work partner was to remain undimmed. For 15 years, he said, she was the most talented and prolific advertising creative person in Brisbane. They were a good team, making a lot of money for a lot of companies. It may have masked what was happening outside of the work environment. Things were considerably less easy there.

To the outside world, Tony and Katie Dell appeared a successful and happy couple but they were enduring a private pain during the first years of their marriage: the struggle to have the children they so desperately wanted.

Years later, Tony Dell would set some of his memories to paper. Those notes, updated every now and then, were initially an attempt to make sure that he would not remain a mystery to the future generations of his family, as he believed his father had. But they also paint a picture of the heartache he and Katie suffered in their attempts to have children. After buying a house in the Wellers Hill neighbourhood, using a war service loan available to him, Katie fell pregnant. Dell remembered that a female colleague at work had come down with German measles and the fears of the rubella virus on an unborn child confronted them with a dilemma: 'All of a sudden we were faced with the terrible decision to terminate. It seemed a simple decision at the time.' They were confident, he said, that they would soon get pregnant again. It proved to be much harder than either of them imagined.

Years later he recalled the miscarriages that followed. At first, like many other veteran families, the couple blamed Agent Orange, the defoliant used by the US in Vietnam which had been linked with birth defects and miscarriage. After tests ruled out any chemical cause, the couple were still unable to conceive. In the place of children, they bought a St Bernard dog and then another one to keep it company, puppies that grew into giants who terrorised the neighbourhood. It was only after the couple had applied for and been accepted as prospective adoptive parents that Katie did fall pregnant again. The sheer relief that adoption might gift them a family, they believed, had eased the pressure and allowed nature to take its course. Their daughter Josephine was born in 1981. A son, Barney, would follow in 1984 and Genevieve, known as Minnie, in 1986. 'These events made the 80s the most memorable decade ever.'

But, in reality, the alarm bells in the relationship had been ringing almost from the beginning, certainly for Katie. Just a few years after the couple tied the knot, her parents became ill. Tony had appeared to be the perfect supportive husband in those difficult times, even carrying his frail father-in-law to and from bed. He had been close to Hector, a man who had endured the ravages of war himself, and they had spent happy times together at the family's home by the sea. But when Hector died in 1978, Dell always said he refused to attend his funeral. 'I'd lost a few mates in Vietnam and I'd seen an awful lot of dead and blown-up bodies and it sort of puts you off for a while and I got sort of blasé about dead people. When I got back to civilian life I used to get embarrassed about not looking sorry and not being able to show the right emotion.'

But Dell's daughter Genevieve tells a different version of the story, as related by her mother. 'He came to the funeral but stood at the back of the church,' she said. For a grieving and emotionally raw Katie it was 'a slap in the face, a real eye-opener'. Dell himself admits he failed his wife at the worst possible moment, that she needed more than he could offer. 'It's hard to explain and she thought I was a bastard and didn't care. I did care. I just couldn't show it.'

It is easy to see now how the demands of normal, civilian life could clash with the damage of war experiences. Then, his way of dealing with these sensitive issues and difficult questions made matters worse: he would just walk away.

'She would always scream, "You're an unfeeling, cold-hearted bastard,"' Genevieve remembers. 'She would also tell him: "That war messed you up."' The incident at her father's funeral was not an isolated one. In losing two younger brothers to suicide and cancer, his parents, his mother-in-law and father-in-law and his two best friends, Dell says he has never shed a tear. He can list the movies, from *You've Got Mail* to *Bohemian Rhapsody*, that will leave him bawling in front of the television screen but the loss of those close to him does not register in the same way. 'Death and destruction became almost normal. I just don't grieve like other people.'

The emotional disconnect between their parents was to be a constant for Genevieve and her siblings. 'Mum lost her temper because she was a very emotional person and was trying to relate to someone who stayed away from emotion; she was very loving and he couldn't offer up love, he was cold and matter-of-fact. It was like getting blood from a stone to get love from someone who could not be present. She would try and try to get him to show love and affection and he would miss the cue time and time again.'

All three children were born in different houses and the family's moves through the 80s told the story of growing prosperity. From a 'tree house' in Bardon, not ideal with its 20ft-high verandahs for a family with a crawling baby, to a home back on that childhood street of Cavendish Road in Coorparoo, where the dogs menaced the passing trolley buses once too often, and then to a sprawling home on the Rathdonnell estate in the leafy suburb of Auchenflower. It was fun but costly, an ambitious move that was to give rise to the beginnings of the financial stresses that would add extra stress to their marriage. 'We were adventurous and forever looking to make a squillion,' said Dell.

Tony Dell never could pinpoint the moment the dark side of his personality began to impact his marriage. Team-mates on the cricket field had seen the growing intolerance. It was only natural that the brooding would carry over into his home life. It is not clear even if he had any idea of where the root of his troubles lay.

At some point though, the arguments began. Time and again Dell would walk away from these fights, leaving the problems unresolved and Katie increasingly frustrated. Even in his later years, Dell refused to take the blame. He pointed to his wife's drinking, for being too doting on their children, even to issues from her childhood and first marriage. To a large extent though, through the successful years of the 1980s, they kept those struggles behind closed doors. In fact, come the end of the decade they had plenty of reason to feel optimistic. Out of the ruins of being fired and partnerships failing, they had built a booming new business. They had bounced back. 'We spent more than we made but we had a good time doing it.'

And then it all came crashing down. For everything that had gone right in the 1980s, something went spectacularly wrong in the 1990s. It began during the Queen's birthday long weekend

Chapter 5

in June 1990, when Dell received a phone call. A major business partner, in whom he had built trust and huge financial liability, had gone bust. Money that had been promised would never materialise and Dell was left with massive debts. He had been promised the earth and, as he kept on believing those promises, he slipped deeper into the mire. His family saw that his own sense of duty in doing the right thing was making matters worse. He fought on, confident his suppliers would stand by him, that being honourable would win out. It was a forlorn hope and flawed plan. All the promises that the money would be paid were empty. In the end the debts ran into the hundreds of thousands. 'It was a harrowing period and it took its toll on all of us.'

That toll was greatest on the family and on Katie in particular. 'She blamed me for us going belly-up and things were never really the same. From then on in, I was the bad guy.' The couple's children were also affected. Dell admits he could be short-tempered with them, such was the focus on financial survival. He admits he was far from fun to be around. 'I reckon I was a crap father in those days.'

It is precisely how his daughter Genevieve remembers it. 'We weren't afraid of him but you didn't want to piss him off. He would go off, a really bad temper. At the same time, he'd come and apologise and tell you that he loved you. You just didn't want to upset him, it was frightening. Everyone at school knew my dad was scary – when I had mates over they knew that you didn't want to piss Tony Dell off.'

As the family's perilous financial situation worsened, keeping his children in their private school became a struggle. They were aged nine, six and four when things started to unravel. Dell says he was being chased by school authorities for outstanding fees, something he managed to keep from his wife. Every now and then, he said, someone would suddenly pop up and ask for the money owed from 1990. It was a fight simply to stay afloat during that dark decade and for years it remained a wonder to Dell how the family made it through.

It was a shattering comedown from the highs; from the big spending, the big house, the big swimming pool in the backyard, the Jaguar for him, the little black sports car for her, the parties, the dinners, to a life shuttling from 'depressing' rental to rental. To Dell, it was nothing short of a failure on his part. Genevieve remembers: 'It was tough because you didn't want to tell your friends why you were moving every six months, you always had to have some cockamamie reason for it. On the drive home, Mum would tell us, "Don't upset your father today, be on your best behaviour." A seven-year-old can't comprehend or understand that finances are dire but it was just pretty full-on.'

The house was sold, so too the business premises they owned, but the price of property was plummeting. The Jaguar went into storage, simply too expensive to run. The marriage was going too, slowly downhill, a fractured and unhappy relationship.

The children were eyewitnesses to this crisis. 'We now know all he was trying to do was restore the family and this superficial wealth. Mum would always say that it was Dad's fault, he was too trusting; she always warned him not to be so trusting. But it came over as unforgiveness and it maybe emasculated Dad a bit. They were fighting like cats and dogs. But I would hear him on the phone begging for business and I could hear the emotion in his voice and it was heartbreaking.'

Chapter 5

That stress and the tension was creeping into every corner of the marriage. The couple were no longer sleeping together. Dell said his sex drive had become non-existent. 'It got worse and worse in my marriage until it got to the point of nothing. I didn't push it or press it. I just lost interest and didn't think about it. I think it had a little bit to do with my lack of confidence in my ability.' When their children realised that Mum and Dad were sleeping in separate beds, Genevieve said, they knew there was no way back for the marriage.

The cracks had developed into a full-blown disintegration and it was only the welfare of their children that kept them together. 'There was no way in the world that we could live separately and give the kids the best chance they could get.' So, they battled on together, through the animosity and the raging arguments, Katie demanding resolution and answers – Tony, unable to provide either, simply walking away. He was never aggressive towards her, he said, but he could not handle what was happening. The problems got bigger as Dell sought a way out. 'All I can remember from when we went belly-up was that I just had this incredible knot in my gut. For years, it was "what do I do now?" and "how do I get out of this?" I was aching for any sort of eventuality that could get us out of it.'

Katie was struggling too. Genevieve remembers her mother's fondness for a casual, social drink in the evening had grown into a more serious and regular habit. The gentle woman who would make her husband a cup of tea and hug him from behind was watching her closest friendship fall apart. 'Some parents might have hidden it from their kids but we were right there with them.'

Through all of this torment, it is unclear that Tony Dell ever questioned whether the blame really rested with his experiences in Vietnam. So much of what was going on in that crumbling marriage is now seen as the classic symptoms of the effects of trauma. The inability to talk problems through, shutting down and walking away, letting the wound fester rather than seeking treatment. There was also that old hangover from army life, of loyalty and doing the right thing by those around you, driving him on, looking for a legitimate way out of the worsening financial mess, rather than taking the easy and perhaps dishonourable route.

It was only when he revisited those notes on his past that Tony Dell saw the unmistakable fingerprints of post-traumatic stress all over his life story. By then he had a diagnosis to his name and looked back in some wonder: 'I find it interesting that I kept writing about PTS symptoms without realising what they were.' He came to believe the breakdown of his marriage was, in part at least, down to that condition. He could see the signposts along the journey downward, far too late of course, and the cost that went with it. Among those costs was the regret that his children missed out on the sort of parental encouragement he wanted to give them.

Without that knowledge though, he was struggling to keep it together as a new century dawned. He described himself as mentally drained, his fight almost gone, but without the option of giving in. There was no way he could curl up and do nothing. He was never someone who could have resorted to drink, he was 'a two-pot screamer'. It would never have occurred to him that taking his own life was a way out. He decided the only way to stay afloat was to keep his mind and body active. He had to find a new direction.

One distraction from the problems – what he called his saving grace – was rediscovering a love of cricket. It was to prove to be a bonding experience with his son. Success as a coach to Barney and his friends took him away from the stresses of work and home. In 2001, Dell took a team of young cricketers on a tour of England and Wales. It was the first time he had returned to home shores since leaving for Australia 42 years earlier. The success of the 'Down-unders' on that tour sparked the germ of an idea for the new start he wanted. Dell called it the Australian International Sports Academy, exporting the country's reputation for sporting excellence to the mass markets of Asia.

The first stage was bringing groups of young people to Queensland to learn from specialist coaches. India was the key to the project, with its economic growth soaring, the middle class booming, sports-mad youngsters and parents with money to burn. The idea grew, with plans to build three multilevel indoor sports centres, solving the twin problem of a lack of space and long rainy seasons in one swoop. His old Queensland captain Greg Chappell joined him in India, a cricketing legend to add superstar weight to the project. Unfortunately for Tony Dell, Chappell's allure was too much for the Board of Control for Cricket in India and they snapped him up to coach the national team. It was an enormous blow to Dell, another hopeful dawn that proved to be false. Not long after came the global financial crisis of 2008 and the whole project was left in ruins. That new direction proved to be a dead end. 'Here I was in another black hole.'

Things were going from bad to worse back home as well. Having moved from Brisbane to the Sunshine Coast in the hope the sports academy would take off, Tony and Katie Dell finally separated. The effect of a marriage falling apart, financial problems and the search for some sort of salvation left Dell feeling beaten. He ended up, where his old schoolfriend Ross Johnston found him, living in the garage of his mother's home.

Dell's parents had moved to Sydney while he was away in Vietnam. His dad had left the world of vacuum cleaners to take a job with a sweets manufacturer – 'all that free chocolate' – and then on to live in South Australia. In their later years, they floated in and out of their son's life but, through the lens of his own struggles with the impact of war, Dell began to reassess a dad who came and went from his own life. 'When I compare his life with mine, I realise that he too could have suffered with PTS, from being caught in the middle of World War Two as a 20-year-old. So many of the things that we thought were odd or antisocial could have been symptoms of PTS.' Dell's mother used to tell her son, 'You're just like your father.' Years later he came to understand what she meant; something he had always denied perhaps did have some merit after all. His parents' deaths, as for most people, must have been felt deeply but Dell said he could not express those emotions. 'I have talked often about my inability to cry in the face of the death of a loved one. I just don't.'

He had been living apart from his wife for seven years when, in June 2012, Katie died. Her daughters found her in bed with her dogs Puddles and Manny by her side. Her estranged husband arrived within the hour. 'He lay in bed with me and my sister all night as we were howling,' said Genevieve. 'He realised it was the loss of the person we were most close to in our childhood and that he had to be more present.' Dell's memory of those days? 'It was just something that happened. Death, as I've said, I'm inured to it.'

The couple's children were close to their mother. 'She was beautiful,' says Genevieve. 'She was a knockout, very emotional, very creative, very clever.' It is evident that some bitterness towards her father remains: 'His illness gives him the luxury of saying he doesn't remember but I know he absolutely regrets what happened. She died in bed with two dogs, not with her husband, in a rental property. This woman who was so gifted and celebrated in her life, so clever, so talented, had died with not much to show for it.'

The memorial service Dell arranged at the Gabba, she believes, reflected what he really felt. Katie had tired of the cricket scene early in the marriage, Genevieve said, so her mum may not have wanted a memorial service to be at a cricket ground. 'But he got the best room, he did what he could, he gave her an amazing send-off. It would have made her happy.'

Many years after Katie's death, Tony Dell struggled to put into words what had drawn him to her all those years ago. Beyond her friendliness, her nice eyes and demeanour. He also remained content to pass some of the blame for their failed marriage to her. But those notes on his life story, written years before, tell a different tale. They were words meant primarily for his children, to record for posterity the relationship during those first two decades together. 'Those 20 years together were breathtaking and they obviously would never have happened without her. She added a creative dimension to my life, mentally and physically.'

Everything else in his life, he wrote, paled into insignificance by comparison. He also reflected on how it had all gone so badly wrong. 'I know the relationship with Katie was very ordinary at the end but we do have incredible history. We took some chances in our lives and they worked wonderfully well but then we've been kicked in the arse well and truly on other occasions.'

Genevieve has noticed that her dad speaks differently of her mum now. 'I remember him saying that the first time he saw her she was the most beautiful woman he'd ever seen. When he looks back on the period he loved the most it isn't the 1970s, he talks about the 1980s when she has had babies and was not looking in the best shape of her life, it is when they were successful, knocking it out of the park. I think what he regrets most is the contribution he may have made to her feeling less, denting her confidence. In the 2000s she was so starved of confidence, she couldn't save herself.'

Genevieve believes his true feelings are contained in the eulogy her dad gave at her mum's memorial service. On that day, he told friends and family: 'Katie Dell was a beautiful woman with an amazing mind. She was a loving and sensitive creature who I fell in love with almost at first sight. We had an amazing life together, made even more special by its rockiness. She was magnificent in adversity. This creative genius grabbed a bogan fast bowler by the scruff of the neck and almost made him human.'

It was a relationship, like so many, hit hard by the ravages of PTS. Families have been destroyed by a lurking shadow that no one even knew was there. Tony Dell can tot up the cost: a broken marriage, estrangement from his children, a brooding, troubled life, and, for a long time, no idea of the reason why. There is tragedy that the discovery of the truth came too late to prevent the damage, even if it is possible to put some of the pieces back together. 'My three kids are my three best friends. I talk to them every day and I'm incredibly close to them.'

Not long before Katie died, after a few years of living apart, Katie and Tony had briefly moved back in together. 'They were a partnership,' Genevieve said. 'He would bend over backwards to support her. Loyalty is his greatest trait.'

In the memoir that he once started writing, Tony Dell wrote that he had two major loves in his life – his Vietnam-era girlfriend Shirley and his wife Katie – and that both had ended disastrously. He later edited those memoirs to add a third woman who had changed the direction of his life – even if it took them both decades to realise it.

6

ON A Sunday morning, David Pye drove his daughter to her weekly concert practice. After dropping her off at school, he drove to the car park of a nearby police station, put the barrel of an assault rifle to his chin and pulled the trigger. The 43-year-old had left a tape in the car's cassette player. In the recording, he apologised to his family for what he had done and asked that someone pick up his daughter.

David Pye was a well-known businessman in his community on Queensland's Gold Coast, with a wife and a son as well as his daughter. He was also a decorated Vietnam veteran. For two decades he had wrestled with the psychological impact of the horrors of that war. By that Sunday in June of 1990, he could go on no longer.

A few days after his death, a psychologist and family friend sat down with David Pye's children and told them in graphic detail what had haunted their father. Their mother wanted them to hear the story, to try to make some sense of their loss. The family wanted it all out in the open.

The story of David Pye's suicide was news for a few days in Australia. But what it revealed about the long-lasting scars of

Vietnam on an otherwise successful, normal man was significant. It was a moment that many Australians saw in black and white that a war, albeit a controversial one, that had ended two decades before, was still costing lives. Whether those reading the stories knew or understood what post-traumatic stress disorder was, there was no escaping its graphic and gruesome grip on the lives of thousands of their friends and neighbours. It was to become a step along a path of learning because at the time even many of those who had walked in David Pye's shoes in Vietnam themselves had little idea that they were still carrying the same burden.

As a corporal in Malaya, David Pye had won Australia's second-highest military honour. He had broken cover when his company was under attack, hurling grenades at enemy fighters, killing a dozen of them and saving lives among his own men. As a sergeant in Vietnam, he and his platoon had come across an enemy bunker system. After throwing phosphorous grenades into the bunker, Pye and another soldier jumped in. They found two dead Viet Cong soldiers, both in their early twenties, a dead child and a dead baby. There was also a young woman, with a baby in one arm and an AK-47 in the other.

The family friend, Peter Webber, told Pye's children: 'The mother and baby were burned with phosphorous grenades. They were standing there alive, screaming. She had the AK-47 in her hand ready to blow Dad and the other Digger away. Dad did exactly what any trained soldier does – he lifted his Armalite rifle and shot the woman and her baby.' Pye had only been in Vietnam for three months. Webber, relaying what his friend had told him years later, told the children: 'It was a hell of an experience for them. Some of them would have been saying, "Hey, the Serg put away the woman and the kid," and that would make Dad feel even worse. That was what the war was like – it was horrific.'

The day after the incident in the bunker, Sergeant Pye suffered physical wounds in a Viet Cong attack and was airlifted home. Shortly afterwards he met and married a nurse called Christene. She said he would talk very little about Vietnam but would occasionally tell her he felt guilty for coming home early, that he felt he had let his comrades down. He told his mother-in-law: 'They trained men to kill and when it was all over there should have been some sort of programme so they could get back to civilian life.' It will sound very familiar to anyone who has spent time with veterans like him. It certainly sounded familiar to Tony Dell. David Pye suffered physical pain from the shrapnel wound to his back and exhibited mood swings but he would keep to himself the story of what happened in that bunker for 15 years.

After he finally did open up to Webber, he began to see a psychiatrist and, in the weeks leading up to his death, had appeared relaxed and happy. Two weeks before he died, he and Christene celebrated their 20th wedding anniversary. He bought her a ruby ring. 'I might not be here when it comes to the 40th,' he told her. 'I think he had probably made up his mind then,' she said.

He had been visiting friends in those last few weeks to thank them for all their support. His family didn't learn that until after he had died. After she heard about that cassette recording, his wife searched the house looking for others, in the hope that there would be more words of explanation. There were none. Her husband, police said, had chosen to end his life where he did to save his family the horror of finding his body.

His wife was left in no doubt that the torment of living with the memories of those 48 hours in the jungle had cost her husband his life. She wanted to tell the story after his death in the hope that others would see the signs and get help. She told the *Sydney Morning Herald*: 'If all this had been brought out into the open 20 years ago, David would probably still be here today.' How many times has that sentiment been spoken by families dealing with the psychological traumas of war? David Pye's family described him as 'heroic'. So many men like him marched in a similar silent struggle. Some were lucky, some were not.

At the time of David Pye's death, Tony Dell was living about 60 miles away in the Brisbane suburb of Auchenflower. Another successful businessman with a family, another man carrying the hidden scars of war. Whatever the ups and downs of family and business life, he went on day to day, unaware of the looming shadow of the war.

David Pye's suicide actually came at the midway point of a long, slow period of discovery for Australians. They were just learning some of those hidden secrets of Vietnam. Through the 1980s and 1990s, discussion of PTS or anything resembling it was limited. When it did surface in the public consciousness, the circumstances were usually extreme and devastating.

Seven years before David Pye took his own life, a former soldier walked into a shopping centre in the Melbourne suburb of Greensborough. Trevor Anderson headed to the third floor, to the Brash's music shop where his wife Pam worked. The couple had separated six weeks earlier. Anderson walked through to an office at the back of the shop and had a short conversation with Pam. He then shot her five times. Moments later he turned the gun on her colleague Jan Toll, who Pam had been living with since the separation. He shot her too. Pam Anderson was 26 years old, Jan Toll was 24, and both women died.

Trevor Anderson walked behind a partition and reloaded his .45 calibre revolver. He emerged into the music shop, put the barrel of the gun in his mouth and fired.

That such horror could happen on a Tuesday afternoon, a few days into the New Year of 1983, was shocking but it took place during a remarkable six days of violent crime in Victoria. Nine people murdered in the state in less than a week, seven people escaped from custody over the same time frame. Melbourne's top detective described the festive period that year as 'absolutely phenomenal for violence'.

Amid this carnage, the Anderson killings were notably tragic. On the personal announcements page of Melbourne's *Age* newspaper, the directors of Brash's music shop placed two small, almost identical death notices for Pam and Jan. Their colleagues would sadly miss the 'loved and most respected member of the company' that each had become. Below Brash's notice for Pam Anderson was another, placed by 'A Fry', mourning that 'Trevor and Pam will be sadly missed. Fond memories.' Little space there to reflect on the violence that ended those lives.

But there were other details. Trevor Anderson was a noted boxer. A 6ft 4in light-heavyweight, known as 'Stretch', and good enough to be part of the stable run by Ambrose Palmer, a sporting champion of the 1930s. At Melbourne's Festival Hall in April 1969 Anderson had won the Australian light-heavyweight title. It was the last win of his career, in part because Trevor Anderson had apparently received the call for another sort of fight altogether.

Chapter 6

The news coverage of the music shop murder-suicide reported that Anderson was a Vietnam veteran. Within 36 hours of the killings, the Vietnam Veterans' Association had asked the Australian government to investigate the cause of 17 suicides it said it had recorded among veterans in the preceding 12 months. The association believed more, perhaps as many again, had gone unreported. The case of Trevor Anderson had been the final straw. The national president of the association, Phil Thompson, said there was an urgent need to find out the cause of the suicides and for government money to extend a counselling service for Vietnam veterans.

That call was a landmark moment. More than a decade after the last Australian soldier had come home from Vietnam, this was the first time that the cry for help, however understated, had finally reached the ears of a nation. It was January 1983, and the media's attention had finally been drawn to the ongoing cost of a war that ended ten years earlier.

There is an added peculiarity to the fact that it was Trevor Anderson's murderous act that prompted this call. Just a day after the veterans' association plea to the federal government, the acting minister for veterans' affairs revealed that, despite all the news reports, Anderson had never served in Vietnam. He had been called up but was declared medically unfit and rejected. It is not clear how the legend of Trevor Anderson as a Vietnam veteran started. Perhaps it was born out of that trope perpetuated in popular culture that all haunted, desperate men were carrying a darkness from somewhere and Vietnam was the most likely source. But wherever it came from, there is no doubt Anderson's story had at last begun a serious conversation. Even so, as David

Pye's death seven years later would demonstrate, it was to be a long, complicated and costly conversation.

Phil Thompson's campaigning work for the Vietnam Veterans' Association had already made him, in the words of one newspaper, 'the veterans' general'. Others talked of an obsessive zeal in a career soldier who had served two tours in Vietnam himself and saw sooner than most the problems soldiers experienced when they came home. He saw marriages breaking up, financial difficulties and mental health problems, and he saw soldiers taking their own lives. He had already spearheaded the campaign for compensation for soldiers who had been exposed to chemical agents used by US forces to defoliate the Vietnamese jungles. Today the effects of Agent Orange are far more clearly understood. The government of Vietnam says some three million people have suffered illness as a result of exposure, the impact far from confined to America's enemies. Tens of thousands of US and Allied troops have claimed disabilities caused by Agent Orange and the wrangle over liability and compensation has lasted decades. Phil Thompson's campaign led to the establishment of the Evatt Royal Commission. In 1985 it reported back that it could find no link between illness and toxic chemicals like Agent Orange. The unrelenting Thompson immediately began his rebuttal case and led the Australian participation in a class action lawsuit against chemical manufacturers.

Agent Orange was blamed for more than physical disorders. In 1981 a coroner in Darwin found that a Vietnam veteran called Lester Reidlinger had shot and killed himself and his wife Ivy because he was likely to have been 'suffering from some malady of mind or body that he felt might stem from Agent Orange'.

Chapter 6

The coroner said he could find no basis for Reidlinger's belief but that it was also unlikely 'that the mere fear or anxiety about being poisoned in Vietnam would have driven him to suicide'. If not that then, what could have cursed a series of Reidlinger's relationships and driven him to end it all in such a bloody way?

Phil Thompson continued to lead the fight for attention on the hidden impacts of the war. He established a crisis counselling hotline and a halfway house for homeless veterans. The fight was a long and hard one. He had once told a friend: 'This is no way to live.'

Every small step along the way meant lives changed and some were undoubtedly saved. Making the Australian public understand was part of the job. If they had been in front of their television sets one evening in April 1983, they may have seen the first major public airing of questions about the psychological impact of the Vietnam War on those who served. This was a couple of months after Phil Thompson's high-profile call for a better government response to the crisis of suicide.

The ABC current affairs series *Open File* broadcast a prime-time 30-minute programme called *What Was the War Like, Love?* It portrayed the Vietnam veterans as the 'forgotten soldiers, men who fought a war which their country now rejects'. It opened with the familiar, jarring archive footage of the war: jungles exploding into fire, artillery and gun fights, terrified Vietnamese women and children crying and shaking. It catalogues the number who served, died and were wounded, the number 'psychologically affected – unknown'. For some of the soldiers who returned home without injury, the commentary says, 'the nightmare had just begun'.

The programme focused on a meeting of veterans at a centre in Sydney, part of the counselling service founded by the veterans' association the previous year. The men who come for help 'very often haven't spoken about Vietnam to anyone before coming in'. Their condition is given a name: post-traumatic stress disorder or delayed stress reaction. The progress made by the men who choose to attend is evident.

We are told that Paul Huggins served in Vietnam in 1966. He smiles softly as he lists the routine horrors he faced. Searching Vietnamese graves for weapons or food supplies, he said, taught you to be cunning and always break into the coffin 'at the foot end'. He chuckles before his face drops. 'Jesus,' he mutters.

He returned home from Vietnam to a job in a bank. 'When the other staff had gone home, I'd sit in the strong room and suck on the bank's revolver,' he said. 'At the time I thought it was quite normal and I did it for years, honestly believing that a lot of other people were sitting around sucking on revolvers too. When I found out that other people weren't, that's when I really started to think I was going crazy.' He twitches, blinking repeatedly, chews on his lip and drags on a cigarette. What had the counselling service done for him? 'I realised I wasn't alone. I wasn't crazy. It is teaching me to get over the guilt I felt. I'm learning you don't have to go around destroying things all the time, destroying relationships, destroying yourself.' Had he not found that service, he said, he 'would have ended up sucking on a revolver once too often'.

Bob Davidson talks of the nightmares, three or four a week for 13 years, vivid and horrifying and very real. In one, he said, he hits a man repeatedly with a tomahawk and then tears his heart out with his hands. All the violence and destruction had left him with a paranoia, he was consumed with death. He had nearly succeeded in drinking himself to death and he feared he would either kill himself or others. Counselling had seen him cut his drinking by half. It had also made him realise that in Vietnam he had been nothing but a 'terrified little boy'.

Among themselves in the group counselling room they can talk openly about their emotions: pain, fear and much more. One man, not named in the programme, tells the group: 'If I've got an anger, and it's a very real anger, it's that no one, be it politicians, the military hierarchy, or the civilians back home, no one asked me about it. They let me come home with a head full of bad feelings and no one gave a damn, and no one does give a damn. The only people who give a damn are in this room. Even my own family is conditioned not to ask. So here I am 13 years later screwed up to the eyeballs, 10 or 12 years of leading a life of hell, because I was never reconditioned to civilian life, never ever deprogrammed. I was never allowed to get that stuff out. I will one day let that anger out against the system.'

It is a clear summation of what thousands were feeling, frustration expressed so well and so calmly, a man who had got used to forcing it down inside, but terrified that a boiling point would one day come.

For a country that had heard little of the internal wounds of the war, it was shocking viewing. The programme would be broadcast a number of times over the next 18 months, edging the stories of those men a little further into the public consciousness. Plenty of Australians knew someone who had served but very few knew what those men were experiencing.

The most harrowing story in the *Open File* programme was that of a man who, it seemed, was not taking advantage of any counselling. Bill Genninges had served two tours in Vietnam, coming home first in 1967 and then again in 1969, to a very different public reception each time. The first return saw a ticker-tape procession through the streets of Sydney and free drinks down the pub. The second, he said, saw him punched in the face for wearing his uniform on the street.

More distressing was what he did in Vietnam. Waking early one morning, he said, he heard the patter of feet on the trail near an ambush point. He saw figures etched against the faint light of the dawn and opened fire. 'I blew away a few people. I should have waited, or should have yelled out, but I didn't know what to yell out, so I just let rip. And there's three people that's dead now that shouldn't be dead.' There is a long pause and Bill swigs from a beer can. He can't say now, he says, whether he fired out of anxiety, stupidity, lack of training or just being psyched up. But when he went to look for the people he had shot, 'They weren't there anymore. They were just lumps of flesh.' For much of the interview, Bill has been looking down or away from the interviewer. Now he fixes him with a haunted look. 'It was a woman, a baby and a little kid. And they're gone. Gone for good. Now, what am I? In the right or the wrong or what? And I have been living with that for 15 years.' He says he struggles to sleep, sweats all night even in winter and has dreams in which he is right back in that jungle. He points to his head: 'The war movies are in there,' he says. They are playing on a loop.

Bill Genninges makes no effort to hide his distress or the big, recurring thought running through his entire story: 'No one is giving any help at all.'

Chapter 6

The very title of the programme – *What Was the War Like, Love?* – comes from a comment made by an aunt of Father Terry Duggan after he came home. 'What could you do?' he asked. 'Scream? How could they tell anyone? The only people they could talk to were the fellows who had experienced the same thing.'

What we don't see in that programme are any wives or partners. It is not made clear if any of the men who are featured have someone at home, fighting their own fight with these scars. There is no mention of the toll being inflicted on anyone close by.

In 1985, the psychologist Ruth Perkins was director of the Vietnam Veterans Counselling Service. She described the problems facing those living with a veteran: 'The army develops that feeling of machismo – you're not supposed to be sensitive and vulnerable so a lot of them lost that emotion, which was replaced by an emotional numbness. Some said they felt dead inside, and had difficulty making emotional commitments. This meant they became cut off.'

An article in *The Age* in Melbourne from that year tells the story of Mick Scrase and the 'mental merry-go-round which has not stopped since he returned from the war. It is as if Vietnam triggered a shot inside his skull which is still ricocheting around in there 15 years later.' The story is familiar: barely any sleep, his wife and parents complaining about his irrational temper and hardness. He and his wife actually did give an interview to their local newspaper, about the fights and violence that had become the norm since his return. They hoped it would help other veterans going through similar things. All that happened was that friends drifted away and wanted nothing to do with them. They endured eight years of misery with no idea it was not normal. 'I didn't know that until about five years ago. A lot of things I was doing I wouldn't even admit to until five years ago: going off into rages, punching holes in the walls at home. I never punched her, I'm glad to say, but I took it out on the furniture, took it out on myself. I've pushed her around, pushed her over furniture, slapped her, that sort of thing.'

He was eventually persuaded to attend one of those early counselling sessions. Until he did, he said, he never realised that others were going through exactly the same thing. Still, two nervous breakdowns and a suicide attempt followed, his wife leaving him in the midst of it all. When he was released from hospital, the couple did get back together and resumed married life. Mick Scrase said working to help other veterans kept him going. This reporting of the couple's story is unusual for its time in that it does feature the experience of his wife. Plenty of others were suffering in the same way.

In his book *The Vietnam Years*, Michael Caulfield relates the stories of a number of Australian war wives who recall living with the ghosts of Vietnam. 'You could never pick it,' said Marjorie Stevens. 'It was like an explosion. Ninety-nine per cent of the time he'd be fine but then he'd go off for no reason.'

By the early 1980s the country had a small band of women who were leading the fight for greater understanding and support. If their work went largely unheralded, it provided perhaps the greatest comfort to the wives and families of veterans. Sandra Adams's husband Gary had been a placid, easy-going mechanic before going to Vietnam. They married soon after he returned. 'When Gary got back from Vietnam, he'd just fly off the handle, over some little thing. I couldn't understand it. I'd blame myself.

Chapter 6

I'd think, "What have I done this time?" He really believed he was going insane.' Gary's headaches and rashes, the couple believed, were linked to exposure to herbicides in Vietnam but there was a heavy psychological impact too and Gary Adams twice attempted suicide.

By day, Sandra worked as a secretary of the Sydney branch of what was then called the Vietnam Veterans' Action Association, led by Phil Thompson and staffed by a network of volunteers across the country. By night, though, Sandra became a helpline counsellor to hundreds of women. There were so many calls she had to instal an extra telephone line at home. She would sit and listen for hours to women telling stories of men who had changed, now depressed, angry and unpredictable. She wanted those women to know they were not alone. 'It is essential to have someone to relate to, who knows what you're going through,' she said. The pleas for help were relentless. 'Sometimes I feel like screaming. I hear the phone and will it to shut up. Then I start talking and I know it's all worthwhile if I can just help one person. Things like having the ironing done become less important.'

The membership was growing and Sandra realised the country was facing a crisis that was being ignored. 'The guys didn't come home as heroes. It was the first war like that. No one wanted to know. They got used to bottling it all in. There are lots of marriage breakdowns. Often the women just want to put it behind them too.'

The denial was just as dangerous. 'One veteran rang because his wife begged him to. I asked him if he ever felt very upset and he said not really. It turned out he'd just broken his wife's jaw.'

Sandra and her husband had poured thousands of dollars of their own money into the association, as calls for government help went unanswered. 'You have to do what you can,' she said.

Some volunteers had training in psychology that they could call on to help with counselling. Carla McCallum's knowledge came at a price. She had become interested in psychology after her Vietnam veteran husband was committed to a psychiatric hospital in the 1970s. The lack of financial help, she said, was crippling the effort to help other veterans. 'We are stretched too thin. We could use money to help train people, to bring others in from country areas, to pay someone to organise it full-time. We just react to crises when we can get to them at the moment. It's no fun arriving at 2am and seeing a grown man curled up on the floor crying.'

Those calls, both women said, were from people who were desperate. Neither pretended to have the answers but their country, they believed, was refusing to even listen to the questions. Families were being destroyed and the nation was offering a collective shrug.

Some were without even the support of a family. For every story of Vietnam-driven family strife, there is another of veterans slipping away into oblivion. Through the 1970s and 1980s, everyone knew someone like that. Tony Dell did. He talks of one, 'a country boy' who went from Vietnam back to the farm and 'got pissed six nights a week – it hit him hard. He was badly affected.' Dell's efforts to keep in touch went unanswered. 'I knew one fella who knew him fairly well and he spent time with him and he said he was just a mess.' Another man, who had been in training with Dell and ended up in the same battalion, also came home and found solace in the bottle. 'He was out in the country and the end result was he got so pissed one day he fell off his horse and killed himself.' These had been close friends in Vietnam.

'Enjoy the war,' went a common joke among German troops in World War Two, 'because the peace will be terrible.'

For many who served in Vietnam it was a chilling truth. Many never really experienced peace again.

In November 1986, Phil Thompson, one of the outstanding voices in the fight for recognition of the problems facing veterans, put the issue firmly back in the headlines.

On a windy night he drove out to an army base in the Sydney suburbs. He knew the place well; he had been an instructor there for five years after coming home from Vietnam. On this Friday, he attached a hose pipe to the car's exhaust, ran it through the window and quietly asphyxiated in the driver's seat. He left no note. Phil Thompson was 42 years old and had been fighting cancer – not caused, he said, by any chemical exposure in Vietnam – and friends said the weight of his campaigning work, that quest for fairness for old soldiers, was wearing him down. 'I think he decided to call it quits because it got too much,' his friend Colin Evans said at the time.

The manner and location of his death was not lost on those close to him. 'His death highlights everything he said about the high suicide rate among veterans,' said the New South Wales president of the veterans' association. 'When the national president does the same bloody thing, it backs up what we've said for years.' The former president in New South Wales added: 'It is tragic for the association that someone has to do as Phil has done to draw attention once again to the Vietnam veterans' cause. There is a message that he took his life near his former army base.' Many saw it as an inspiration to keep on fighting.

7

THE TELEPHONE call came out of the blue. It was the winter of 2007 and, until that moment, Tony Dell had no idea that he was the only Test cricketer to have served in combat in Vietnam. The man who told him, a retired colonel, thought that piece of history made Dell the perfect guest at the first-ever International Defence Cricket Challenge that summer. Teams from the Australian Army, Navy and Air Force were due to compete with defence forces from New Zealand and the United Kingdom in Canberra.

Dell was in his early sixties, living in the garage of his mother's house on the Sunshine Coast and in a physical state bad enough to worry his old mates. He had no money. Baked beans on toast constituted a good meal. A concoction of chicken nuggets in chicken noodle soup was a treat. 'I was living off the smell of an oily rag,' he said. He had never much bothered with the traditions of being a military veteran. He had never taken part in the annual ANZAC Day parades, never went to reunions, never wanted to return to Vietnam, as so many had done, to revisit the old haunts and try to heal the old wounds. His war service seemed an age away to him. It had left no scars, he thought. No physical ones, anyway. But an event combining military service and cricket intrigued him. He said 'Yes' and flew to Canberra.

He stayed for the final three days of the tournament, watching the semi-finals and final at the Manuka Oval. The other guests included the commanding officer of the first Australian Services side, moulded from soldiers, sailors and airmen still left in Europe at the end of World War Two in 1945. They played so-called Victory Tests to packed English grounds, war-weary cricket fans crying out for a bit of normality, the familiar routines of peacetime life. That first services team knew plenty about combat and cricket. In the team was Flying Officer Keith Miller, who would go on to be regarded as his country's greatest cricketing all-rounder.

At that first International Defence Cricket Challenge, Tony Dell was the sole representative from the Vietnam War. As he was preparing to leave Canberra for home, someone asked in passing if he had received the fifth medal due to Vietnam veterans. The fifth medal was news to him: he didn't even have the four he was originally issued with. 'I told them my kids had wrecked them over the years, tearing the ribbons off, and that I had nothing left.' He was told he could request replacement medals from the Department of Defence. He nodded, said he would, flew home and promptly forgot all about it. 'I got a call a month later. "Have you been back to get your medals?" I said no. They called in January. "Have you been back?" "No," I said. I thought to myself I'd better do it otherwise they'll just keep on calling and it'll drive me nuts.'

Half an hour up the Sunshine Coast from Caloundra is the glistening seaside suburb of Maroochydore. 'Pulsing with nightlife, full of bloodthirsty adventure and oozing with soul' says the tourist blurb. Tony Dell went looking, not for any of that, but for the veterans' drop-in centre. He found it upstairs in the Cotton Tree library. As he began to explain why he was there, looking for information on applying for replacement medals, the volunteers wanted to talk about cricket instead. Over a cup of tea, the conversation flowed, old veterans chewing over the past, and after half an hour of chatting, they delivered a bombshell.

'They said, "You have PTS,"' remembers Dell. 'Like all soldiers who think they are bulletproof, I said, "Bullshit."'

Until that moment, Dell has said, he was unaware that PTS even existed. Sure, he had seen fellow veterans who had turned to drink or drugs to cope with their demons. 'You weak bastards,' he would think. This, though, was his own moment of truth. Perhaps surprisingly, after that initial moment of shock and denial, he said he accepted what the volunteers were telling him. They had been through war themselves, they had been diagnosed with PTS and had learned to live with it. They wanted to help others. Whatever it was that they saw in Dell, they were in no doubt.

The experts say PTS can be difficult to spot. Symptoms can appear months or years after the traumatic events; sufferers may believe they have healed themselves. But it can fester away, looking like depression or rage, and having an impact on everything from sleep to relationships. Doctors say sufferers feel emotions more intensely and they can react unpredictably to seemingly normal circumstances – angry and irrational behaviour can erupt out of nowhere. It can be hard for sufferers to concentrate and they feel danger where there is none. Life can be consumed by hopeless thoughts, negativity, guilt and shame. Things that once brought joy are no longer enjoyable. Sufferers avoid people, even people not necessarily connected with the traumatic event, and that leaves them detached from society. In the Cotton Tree library that day, Tony Dell ticked most of the boxes. 'They picked it up from some of my answers, the way we talked; they knew the pertinent questions and I obviously gave the right answers.' He was in fact a textbook case of PTS.

At that stage he knew very little about what his diagnosis would mean for him, beyond the likelihood of a much-needed military pension. But he did start to feel just a flicker of relief, a sense that, just possibly, here was something to arrest the downward spiral in his life. 'I had lost the will. I had always been a fighter but I had lost the fight. My marriage was going downhill slowly, and I didn't know what I was going to do with myself.'

More practically, the next step was an appointment with a psychiatrist to confirm the diagnosis. Then came the precious 'White Card' from the Department of Veterans' Affairs. It granted the holder free medical treatment and care. The first thing Tony Dell did with his was undergo knee replacement surgery. 'At that point I couldn't stand for more than 60 seconds, couldn't walk a hundred metres.'

While he was still recovering from surgery, he was called to a review board to assess whether he was eligible to be upgraded to the coveted medical 'Gold Card'. Hobbling in on crutches, meeting a doctor who was also a cricket fan, clearly did the trick. The Gold Card arrived two days later. 'They called it the magic card; flash it and you get full medical and dental, all paid for.'

Chapter 7

Dell had struggled with health issues for years. The knee and shoulder problems had been there throughout his cricket career. Some of the delights of old age were now creeping up. On a visit to Caloundra, his friend Greg Delaney had noticed that Dell desperately needed reading glasses. 'I said, "Look, I'll go and buy you some," but he wouldn't accept it. It was a big thing to him. Just a definite no. Two weeks later he had his Gold Card and was seeing an optometrist.'

Delaney is one of many who believe that veterans like Dell should have received health care benefits for life the moment they returned from active service. 'He had to fight like hell to get hold of a Gold Card from the mongrels.'

He had certainly struggled to get by without that 'magic' access to healthcare. In 2005 he travelled to Delhi as part of the effort to get the Australian International Sports Academy off the ground. The 15-hour flight there via Singapore was gruelling enough. The return on the same route took its toll. The exit row seat he always tried to secure on long flights was unavailable. When he unfolded himself from a standard seat in Brisbane, though, he felt fine. Two weeks later, all was not well. He had difficulty breathing and an X-ray revealed a blood clot on his lung. Having been told not to drive, he took a taxi back to his doctor who immediately called an ambulance. Diagnosed with deep vein thrombosis, he spent six days in the intensive care unit 'at death's door'. For years it was unclear to him how he managed to pay for the care.

With a pension and healthcare secured, things were looking up. When the International Defence Cricket Challenge came around again, he was invited to give a speech on awards night.

By then he had learned a lot more about his PTS. Sessions with a psychiatrist had identified specific moments which had adversely affected his life. With this new-found awareness, the speech he gave that night earned a standing ovation. As he walked back to his seat, the handshakes, the expressions of thanks, the warmth of the reception was more than just gratifying. It gave him an inkling that this was a significant moment in his life. He was playing a part in breaking down the wall of silence. 'It was taboo to talk about it in defence circles, even in 2009. There was a feeling that it was a sign of weakness, in the military and with first responders, that somehow it would impede your rise in the ranks if you did talk about it; it was all so macho.'

The memory that stuck with him most from that trip was the captain of the New Zealand Army cricket team approaching him. Half the players in the team wanted to talk to Dell about what he had said. 'That was the first indication that I had done something positive and good. Suddenly they thought it was okay to talk about it and open up.' On the flight back to Brisbane, people continued to seek him out and shake his hand. It was a reaction that was to lead to a life-altering decision.

Another of those who heard him give that awards night speech would turn out to be one of his greatest supporters. Like Dell, Angus Houston was born a Brit. In 1968, as Dell was coming home from Vietnam, Houston was swapping south-west Scotland for the remote farming wilderness of Western Australia. That 21-year-old 'jackeroo' would end up as Australia's Chief of the Defence Force. As a helicopter pilot, he had been awarded the Air Force Cross. A decade later, as a senior officer, he was involved in the strategic planning for the Gulf War in 1990. He would go on to plan the ANZAC centenary celebrations in 2011 and receive a knighthood for his service. As a leader of military men and women, Sir Angus was impressed by what he saw and heard in Tony Dell.

'It moved everyone in the room,' he remembered. The crippling effects of PTS, which he saw as having been so often swept under the carpet, were suddenly being laid bare by someone who had been there. 'He was prepared to stand up and talk openly about having PTS. He was very courageous to do that.' The evening ended with Sir Angus offering to do whatever he could to help Dell. The irony was not lost on Dell that here he was, a former National Service private, sitting down with the most senior military figure in the country. But Sir Angus saw that Dell was in a unique position to change not just the military attitudes to PTS but those of the wider community. A former serviceman who had risen to the top as a cricketer and built relationships with some of the biggest names in sport, in a country so defined by sporting excellence, Sir Angus knew Australians would listen to a man like Tony Dell. 'I encouraged him to talk as it was good for him and good for the community. Lots of young people who are diagnosed with PTS feel they can't talk about it. What he did was something that people needed to hear.' The message got through; Dell realised his life story could open doors. He remembers that hug from Sir Angus and congratulations from the chief of the army. 'For the first time someone had come out and said, "I have PTS and this is what it's done to my life."'

He had a more pressing concern when he stepped off the flight back from that speech. He was due to undergo a second knee replacement operation. The toil of his cricket career had continued to ravage his body physically. But, as he lay recuperating from the surgery in a hospital bed, the memories of the reception he had received for his speech swirled in his mind. Throughout his life, he thought, his energy and drive had built careers and, when things had gone wrong, had pushed him to start over and build them again. In PTS, here was a problem of immense proportions and, it was clear to him, a glaring need for someone to do something about it. 'I was in a hospital bed, with nothing to do but be in pain and I thought to myself, I can do something there.' There was another factor: veterans on military pensions are limited in the number of hours they can legally work. For a self-described workaholic, who used hard graft to escape the painful thoughts and emotions, being prevented from working was nothing more than a trap.

Out of that need to work, driven by a nation's need for action, the PTS Foundation Limited was born. It would become better known as 'Stand Tall 4 PTS'. The one thing that had been as shocking as his own diagnosis to Dell was the discovery of how many others were in the same boat. To him the answer was a charity focused on offering support to sufferers, creating more awareness of PTS across the country, reducing the stigma surrounding it and pushing the government to take greater action. Sufferers were caught in a debilitating dilemma: 'PTS is bad enough. It affects people being able to work, their families, their ability to live. But the stigma stops people getting help.' If he could help people recognise PTS in themselves and others and be open to looking for and accepting support, Stand Tall could be a success. He also secured a powerful patron in Sir Angus

Houston. 'Tony was a trailblazer in talking openly about the condition and the journey,' he said.

There was one significant hurdle to setting up a charity: the mountain of debt that Dell had accumulated over the previous two decades. The years of unopened mail meant bills and fines from the tax authorities had gone unpaid. He was $80,000 in the red. His salvation came in the form of his friend Bruce Tanner, a veteran of the party set in early 1960s Brisbane who had somewhat sensibly grown up to become an accountant. Tanner waded through the stacks of yellowing paper, piecing it all together and negotiating with the Australian Tax Office until they eventually ruled there was no case to answer. Tony Dell emerged solvent. He would also have reason to be grateful to the Australian Cricketers' Association for money from its hardship fund to pay off some of his debts and the Kerry Packer Foundation for paying off the rest. Now the work could begin.

In the estimation of the US Department of Veterans' Affairs, about 30 per cent of Vietnam veterans suffer PTS in their lifetime. But spend any amount of time reading the statistics and percentages and it is evident no one really knows the true extent of the problem. Governments can measure diagnoses over a set period, how many people are being treated and the rate of PTS in the military population compared to the civilian one, but the secrets of the mind and how individuals react to trauma makes PTS a difficult condition to measure and manage. Many, like Tony Dell, diagnosed in his sixties, spend decades unaware they were suffering from an actual medical condition at all.

The truth of PTS lies deep inside the complex structures of the brain. Research has identified three areas that appear to be functionally and structurally different in sufferers of PTS compared to non-sufferers. The first is the hippocampus, a part of what's called the limbic system, a set of brain structures that effectively house our emotional lives. Our behaviour, motivation and memory are formed in the limbic system, processing all the input from our sensory systems. Taking its name from the ancient Greek for 'seahorse' because of its physical resemblance, the hippocampus is what consolidates information in the brain, things like short- and long-term memory and the spatial memory that enables us to navigate our way through the world.

The prefrontal cortex is the part of the brain responsible for cognitive behaviour. Our decision-making, the expression of our personality, how we regulate our social behaviour, even our morality is contained there. Studies have shown it to be a key part in reactivating old emotional associations and events, in effect supporting the development of PTS. It also feeds the third part of the brain most affected in sufferers.

The amygdala is what controls our emotional responses like fear, anxiety and aggression. We all have two of them in our temporal lobes, also part of the limbic system. Numerous studies have shown that the amygdalae could be responsible for the extreme emotional reactions in sufferers of PTS.

The reason is that these three areas of the brain, which together help regulate stress but also trigger the typical symptoms of PTS, all suffer lasting damage as a result of traumatic stress. The most significant impact is on the hippocampus. Neuroimaging has revealed that trauma causes a reduction in its volume. Because it is responsible for the recording of memory and differentiating the past from the present and its relation to our surroundings, reduced capacity makes it harder for sufferers to distinguish between the two. This means a new experience or environment can trigger an extreme stress response even if it has nothing to do with the trauma from the past.

The prefrontal cortex has also been shown to be reduced in volume in PTS sufferers, limiting its ability to regulate the emotional responses of the amygdalae. When that happens, those emotional responses like fear and panic go haywire. One piece of research even found that when PTS sufferers were shown photographs of people expressing fear on their faces, their amygdalae tended to have a higher activation than someone without PTS.

As if those changes in the structure of the brain were not enough, PTS sufferers also see an increase in the release of the stress hormones cortisol and norepinephrine, both of which can exacerbate anxiety.

Put simply, the symptoms of PTS are just the behavioural manifestation of those structural and neurochemical changes in the brain's circuits, the neural pathways damaged and reformed by traumatic stress.

It is those outward manifestations that present the daily challenge for sufferers and those close to them. Tony Dell admits his own PTS is 'middle of the range' – he knows that others suffer far worse than him. But the menu of symptoms and side effects is debilitating and life-altering.

Among the most unpleasant are flashbacks. They can come at any time, day or night, sometimes triggered by a sound or a smell, something in the street or on the news, sometimes simply out of nowhere. In the blink of an eye, a sufferer is back at the scene of the trauma, mentally reliving the event that caused the PTS in the first place. Images of what happened float across their mind's eye, the sensations of pain or terror become real all over again, the emotions of that moment as raw as during the event, the distress making their heart race, breath short, the panic gripping the throat. The fear of flashbacks alone can leave sufferers on edge.

The lines between symptoms are often blurred. There is crossover between flashbacks and the condition of hyper-arousal. It is the state of being always on edge, feeling jittery and unable to relax. There is no trigger – it is constant. Sufferers are unable to focus or concentrate, finding eating or even sleeping to be difficult. All of it leaves them stressed and angry. It is exhausting.

Sufferers also talk of hyper-vigilance, scanning the environment for threats all the time, reacting unpredictably, quick to anger or irritability with friends and family. It has been described as that feeling when someone jumps out and startles you, but with PTS it never goes away.

Then come the panic attacks. When the emotion of fear is strong enough to bring on physical symptoms of palpitations, shortness of breath, sweats and shaking, nausea and dizziness. It can feel like a heart attack.

All of these symptoms play a part in sufferers often struggling to sleep. Perhaps they cannot drop off at night; maybe they avoid it because they feel they will be vulnerable to danger while sleeping. Even if they do manage to fall asleep many suffer with terrible nightmares. Like flashbacks, this vivid reliving of traumatic events can cause distress. This all affects the quality of sleep, contributing to exhaustion and health problems.

Those physical ailments often go hand in hand with the psychological impact of PTS. It has been observed that the condition can lead to an increased risk of sufferers developing chronic pain, the cost of stress and exhaustion.

Some symptoms fit into broader categories like depression and anxiety. People with depression have been shown to have an increased risk of PTS and, inversely, people with PTS are more prone to suffering depression. There is a jumble of coping mechanisms that have been identified as familiar to PTS sufferers. They may resort to emotional numbing, the mind shutting down any emotion, reasoning that if you don't feel it then there is no way it can make you suffer. Repression has a similar effect: intentionally blocking memories, throwing themselves into work to keep the mind busy. Alcohol and drugs have been used to a similar end. Avoidance will see a sufferer stay away from situations that might bring back memories of the traumatic event or set off a flashback. Often it means avoiding crowds or even certain people. There can be a feeling or detachment from one's own mind and body. All of this can lead, intentionally or not, to withdrawal and isolation and the subsequent crisis of loneliness. There can be mood swings, drastic changes in behaviour and demeanour. In the background, there can be self-destructive thoughts and even guilt or shame. A sufferer can feel they are somehow responsible for the trauma that started it all in the first place.

It is a sobering list. Of course, not all sufferers experience every symptom and each encounters their own to different degrees. They are also not the only one suffering.

Research has shown the effects of PTS on close relationships to be severe. The mental health of partners and the functioning of families are badly affected. It has been reported that military veterans with PTS are more likely to experience problems with their marriages, relationships and parenting. They are less expressive with their partners than veterans without PTS and more likely to experience anxiety around intimacy. Sexual dysfunction tends to be higher among veterans with PTS, the lack of interest in sex adding to problems in those marriages. In the US, researchers found that more than a third of Vietnam veterans saw their marriages fail within six months of their return. Even more staggering, the rate of divorce was twice as high among veterans with PTS.

Even if they do stay together, research has revealed that families of veterans with PTS are exposed to more family violence and physical and verbal aggression. The severity of the aggression, researchers found, was directly related to the severity of the veteran's PTS symptoms.

As well as feeling compelled to take on more of the household burden, wives of veterans with PTS also felt a responsibility to assume the care of their partner and his medical problems. The feeling of walking on eggshells, acutely aware of the triggers for PTS and possibly explosive reactions, trying to minimise the risk, is what is known as the 'caregiver burden'.

Not surprisingly, the research has discovered that the partners of veterans with PTS were far more likely to develop mental health problems of their own. Wives and partners reported their social relationships had suffered and that they were less happy and satisfied in their lives. About half of the partners of veterans with PTS said they had felt on the verge of a nervous breakdown. The stresses of dealing with a partner with PTS meant their own needs were not being met. With the increased fear of domestic violence, they were suffering a secondary traumatisation, the indirect impact of the trauma on those close to the sufferer.

By the time Tony Dell was embarking on his crusade to help other sufferers of PTS, he knew some of this, a great deal of it from personal experience. What he knew little about was getting a charity off the ground. 'It was hard, slow work and we had no idea where to start.' As he learned more, Sir Angus Houston's advice, to tell his life story to create interest in Stand Tall, was starting to bear fruit. In November 2014 the Australian Prime Minister Tony Abbott wrote to Dell agreeing that the charity would be the official partner for the match between the Prime Minister's XI and the touring England team the following January. News coverage of the announcement featured a photo of Abbott and Dell together with cricketer and former army and air force officer Group Captain Cate McGregor and Australian batsman Michael Hussey. The match itself at the Manuka Oval in Canberra put Stand Tall on the map as a voice for veterans.

The same year Stand Tall staged PTS15, a forum of experts in research, diagnosis and treatment, coming to Brisbane from around the world. Dell described the forum as 'the most significant event in the long history of the disorder. A positive outcome would be that one million sufferers in Australia would no longer feel they have no support.' In his closing speech, Dell vowed it would not be a flash in the pan: 'Too often in the past events like this stagnate after the first bottle of champagne is opened. I promise every Australian living with PTS that this will not happen here.'

In June 2016 Stand Tall staged its most ambitious project yet – the Lightning Bolt convoy, an 11-day journey from Brisbane to Melbourne via Sydney and Canberra, featuring military and first responder vehicles, carrying word of the challenges of PTS directly into communities along the way. News coverage and a social media blitz, Dell estimated, put Stand Tall in front of some ten million people. In September 2017, to coincide with World Suicide Prevention Day, Stand Tall staged its first major public PTS Awareness Day with plans for it to become an annual fixture.

Another forum followed in 2017 and a second Lightning Bolt convoy in 2018, through four states and even crossing the Tasman Sea to New Zealand. It also featured competitors from the Invictus Games, the sports event created by Prince Harry for wounded, injured or sick armed services personnel. The convoy was timed to arrive in Sydney at the opening of the fourth Invictus Games. It was, Dell said, 'without doubt the largest awareness event stage for post-traumatic stress, ever'.

It was also testament to Dell's energy and drive. Even the small team of volunteers that keeps Stand Tall on the road recognised one reality: that Stand Tall was the manifestation of one man's passion. As Tony Dell drove the charity, so it drove him.

He liked to tell the story of his old GP friend John Parker, who regularly took his medical knowledge to war zones as a volunteer with Médecins San Frontières. What Parker saw in Iraq, Afghanistan, Sudan and Congo contributed to his own PTS but, when asked why he carried on in old age, he quoted George Bernard Shaw: 'We don't stop playing because we grow old; we grow old because we stop playing.'

Chapter 7

Dell's determination is to make a difference: 'One veteran tops himself or herself in Australia every day of every year,' Dell told ESPN in 2015. The lack of understanding, the lack of government funding for research and treatment rankled him.

In his quest to know more about PTS, in 2014, Dell became the first of 300 Vietnam veterans to sign up for a new research project. The Gallipoli Medical Research Foundation and the Returned Services League of Queensland wanted to understand the health risks faced by those with PTS, as well as the role of genetics. Half of the veterans who signed up had been diagnosed with PTS. The study was a world first and the results, published in the *Medical Journal of Australia*, were stark. Veterans with a diagnosis of PTS endured poor long-term health and suffered heart disease, gastric complaints and sleep disorders. It will not have come as news to many with PTS.

But how many veterans have lived with undiagnosed PTS? How many have cycled in and out of doctors' offices and hospitals with no answers? How many, like Tony Dell before 2008, are unaware of what ails them? It is why the work to raise awareness remained vital to him.

He had his own near-miss story. In the mid-1990s, when he was living in Brisbane and trying to hold his life together, Dell called in to a veterans' drop-in centre not far from his home. He met someone he had served with in Vietnam. 'He said to me, "Come back in and we can get you a pension and sort things out."' Dell declined, said he was okay and that he would work through it, would get himself on his feet again. A lot happened between that day and 2008. 'I look back and think maybe life would have been totally different.'

8

LIKE MOST people, Tony Dell missed the moment that the term 'post-traumatic stress disorder' was officially born. It was 1980 and few outside of the world of psychiatry took any notice. But, at the urging of a team of researchers, the term made its first appearance in the third edition of the American Psychiatric Association's *Diagnostic and Statistical Manual of Mental Disorders*. DSM, as it is known, is the healthcare handbook for doctors identifying mental disorders. Whether it is the profession's bible or its dictionary, to military veterans from 1980 it was a potential life-saver.

The inclusion of PTS was controversial. Coming so soon after the end of the Vietnam War, many wondered whether it was just a political stunt to soothe anti-war sentiment and guilt over veterans' plight. It was also the first time a mental disorder which was caused by an external traumatic event, outside of the range of usual human experience, had been included. Such events might include combat.

But if the term PTS was born in the 1980s, the condition itself has been with us since the dawn of time. In fact, for thousands of years, wherever combat has taken place, and whenever someone was there to record it, the psychological trauma of warfare has been evident.

For many years, the first eyewitness account of what looked a lot like PTS was credited to the man regarded as history's original historian. The Greek writer Herodotus, reporting on the Battle of Marathon in 490 BC, told the story of the warrior Epizelus.

In the midst of battle, Herodotus wrote, Epizelus 'was fighting bravely when he suddenly lost the sight of both eyes, though nothing had touched him anywhere, neither sword, spear nor missile. From that moment he continued blinded as long as he lived.' In speaking about what happened to him, Herodotus wrote, 'he fancied he was opposed by a man of great stature in heavy armour, whose beard overshadowed his shield. But the phantom passed him by and killed the man at his side.'

It was not unusual for warriors at the time to talk of a 'phantom' on the battlefield. The appearance of gods and heroes was often invoked to explain the emotional toll of war. For centuries the symptoms we now associate with PTS – flashbacks, out-of-body experiences and anxiety – were viewed as the workings of gods or the devil. It was only in the 18th century that the theories of an Austrian physician called Franz Mesmer led to the scientific term 'trauma' taking the place of these spiritual speculations. Mesmer also brought us the theory of illnesses involving internal magnetic forces – he is the reason we have the word 'mesmerise'.

The experience of Epizelus though, struck blind by terror and the sight of seeing his comrade killed, has enough parallels with modern warfare to show that combat stress is nothing new. In fact, we now know that episodes had been recorded hundreds of years earlier even than the Battle of Marathon.

A team of researchers at Anglia Ruskin University have analysed texts from ancient Mesopotamia, written during the Assyrian dynasty as early as 1300 BC. Squeezed between the rivers Tigris and Euphrates and making up what is now modern-day Iraq, the region is regarded as the cradle of civilisation. Among the hundreds of thousands of tablets of text the Mesopotamians left behind, many are medical handbooks and prescriptions, revealing a society that believed in the importance of diagnosis of illnesses. In a dynasty frequently at war, where soldiers would follow a cycle of one year of fighting followed by one year at home, the researchers found most of the texts on trauma were concerned with combat wounds. This gruelling routine of battle exposed the male population to 'significant trauma'.

The medical texts show that men suffered flashbacks, sleep disturbance and depression, often explained away as the spirits of enemies they had killed coming back to haunt them. The texts tell of soldiers whose words were unintelligible for days on end, who roamed aimlessly and fell into depression, gripped by the hand of a roving ghost. 'His mouth is seized so that he is unable to cry out to one who sleeps next to him.' These descriptions of soldiers encountering the ghosts of those they had killed was not confined to ancient history, according to one of the men who led the research. 'That's exactly the experience of modern-day soldiers who've been involved in close hand-to-hand combat,' Professor Jamie Hacker Hughes told the BBC. As a former consultant clinical psychologist to the Ministry of Defence, Professor Hacker Hughes saw a clear lesson: 'As long as there has been civilisation and as long as there has been warfare, there have been post-traumatic symptoms. It's not a 21st-century thing.'

The Assyrian texts revealed something else in common with what we now call PTS: the vivid nightmares suffered by warriors. Horrifying dreams of battle were reported in the writings of Hippocrates, the ancient Greek physician considered to be the father of medicine. The Roman poet Lucretius wrote that 'the minds of mortals often in sleep will do and dare the same'.

Even the Old Testament carried stories of the mental scars of battle. The book of Deuteronomy, believed to have been written in the 7th century BC, records that military commanders were having to rotate soldiers away from the front line because of nervous breakdowns. They even thought such breakdowns might be contagious.

'When thou goest out to battle against thine enemies, and seest horses, and chariots, and a people more than thou, the officers shall say, What man is there that is fearful and fainthearted? Let him go and return unto his house, lest his brethren's heart faint as well as his heart.'

Classic literature has also played its part in opening a window into the past of psychological trauma. Homer's epic poems, the *Iliad* and the *Odyssey*, tell the stories of the trials of Achilles during the last year of the Trojan War and the ten-year journey home of Odysseus after the fall of Troy. His anguish at seeing friends die and the adjustment to civilian life are so familiar and timeless that modern-day American military veterans are now offered the chance to study Homer's words to give meaning to their own experiences in Vietnam, Afghanistan and Iraq.

Few writers have expressed the human condition with as much clarity as William Shakespeare. Not surprisingly, a man whose plays are packed full of battles and bloodshed wrote piercingly on the costs. In *Henry IV, Part 1*, Lady Percy addresses her husband Sir Henry, fresh back from combat and about to leave again:

> Tell me, sweet lord, what is 't that takes from thee
> Thy stomach, pleasure, and thy golden sleep?
> Why dost thou bend thine eyes upon the earth,
> And start so often when thou sit'st alone?
> Why hast thou lost the fresh blood in thy cheeks
> And given my treasures and my rights of thee
> To thick-eyed musing and curst melancholy?
>
> Thy spirit within thee hath been so at war
> And thus hath so bestirred thee in thy sleep,
> That beads of sweat have stood upon thy brow
> Like bubbles in a late-disturbèd stream;
> And in thy face strange motions have appeared,
> Such as we see when men restrain their breath
> On some great sudden hest. O, what portents are these?
> Some heavy business hath my lord in hand,
> And I must know it, else he loves me not.

Those words, written more than 400 years ago, have been called the best description of PTS in the English language.

Even one of the bard's most beloved characters, in one of his most famous speeches, touched on the darkness. Mercutio, in *Romeo and Juliet*, speaks of Queen Mab, the tiny fairy who

creates the dreams in the heads of mortals and is just as capable
of putting bleak nightmares there:

> Sometime she driveth o'er a soldier's neck,
> And then dreams he of cutting foreign throats,
> Of breaches, ambuscadoes, Spanish blades,
> Of healths five-fathom deep; and then anon
> Drums in his ear, at which he starts and wakes,
> And being thus frighted swears a prayer or two
> And sleeps again.

It would be more than 200 years after Shakespeare's time that
science began to wrestle with the causes of these psychological
scars. But if the theories of gods and demons, and even fairies,
were falling out of fashion, there was still room for unusual
explanations of the symptoms we now know as PTS.

Doctors treating casualties of the French Revolutionary and
Napoleonic wars noticed that soldiers were afflicted by near
misses from shells. Out of this grew the theory of 'vent du boulet'
syndrome – literally translated as 'wind of the cannonball'. It took
the death and destruction of two major conflicts in the middle
of the 19th century to see real medical advances begin.

Until the American Civil War and the Franco-Prussian War,
combat trauma was known by a variety of peculiar names. The
Austrian physician Josef Leopold labelled it 'nostalgia' because
sufferers often reported feeling sad and missing home. Others
were diagnosed with 'melancholia', appearing lethargic and
withdrawn. When American Civil War soldiers were studied,
their signs of anxiety were often accompanied by a rapid

heartbeat leading doctors to diagnose a physical cause. This overstimulation of the nervous system, they thought, was down to the heavy packs soldiers carried, homesickness and even a lack of motivation. The cure for what they called 'soldier's heart' was a dose of drugs and a swift return to the front line. This idea that it was a physical injury that led to PTS-type symptoms was reinforced by research in Europe into an even more bizarre theory. The increase in rail travel had led, predictably enough, to an increase in rail disasters. Post-mortem examinations on those who died in train crashes revealed injuries to the central nervous system. But the fact that so many of those who survived showed symptoms of stress baffled doctors. To some of them, the logical conclusion was that those symptoms were caused by the same thing as the physical injuries, a whack to the brain or nervous system. The theory of 'railway spine' persisted for years, even as the evidence was mounting in support of those who saw emotional shock as being responsible.

All of the theorising was doing little to help those suffering as the wars kept on coming.

The American Civil War was the bloodiest war in American history. More died during those four years, three weeks and six days of fighting than in both world wars, Korea and Vietnam combined: a total of more than 650,000 dead, about two per cent of the country's population at the time. Americans went to war with each other at a time when new and catastrophically efficient weapons were available – it was the first modern war. For many of those who survived the slaughter, there was to be little peace afterwards. The scientific knowledge simply did not exist in the 1860s to understand that a traumatic experience could have an impact on the brain. Consequently, doctors saw no connection between combat and the sort of symptoms veterans were reporting. Even the happiest of homecomings would soon fade to be replaced by the unsettling fog of the post-war. At the time, for many who suffered mental breakdowns, the only option was admission to an insane asylum and that is where thousands of Civil War veterans ended up.

Data on the return to civilian life of Civil War veterans is somewhere between patchy and non-existent. But in his book *Shook Over Hell*, the historian Eric Dean lays out the remarkable detail contained in a study of 291 Civil War veterans who were committed to the Indiana Hospital for the Insane. All of those admitted, he points out, were considered curable – chronic cases were routinely turned away. But the range of symptoms and behaviours were typical of modern-day PTS, he wrote, 'including elements of depression, anxiety, social numbing, re-experiencing, fear, dread of calamity and cognitive disorders. Many of these men continued to suffer the after-effects of the war and, along with their families, often lived in a kind of private hell involving physical pain, the torment of fear and memories of killing and death.'

They lived with delusional paranoia, and suicidal thoughts were also common. Dean found that more than half of the residents of one Civil War veterans' home had either tried, succeeded or considered taking their own life.

Newall Gleason had been a successful civil engineer before his commission as a lieutenant colonel. His unit had seen ferocious fighting and, despite his being honoured for his bravery, fellow officers witnessed a slow deterioration in his mental state. He struggled when he returned to civilian life and after a 'three-day episode of violent mania in which he was raving and had to be restrained' he was admitted to the asylum. Staff noticed he was prone to issue military orders, as if in battle. His mental torment continued on his release and, after an evening out with his wife, she awoke to find him standing at the top of the cellar stairs. 'He yelled or screamed at her to leave and plunged headlong down the cellar stairs where he died of a fractured skull.' Newall Gleason's is just one among hundreds of suicides that Civil War researchers have unearthed decades on. It is likely many hundreds more remain buried in the mists of history. Thousands more veterans simply struggled on, bearing the burdens themselves. As with veterans of many a conflict before and since, they felt there was a stigma with mental illness. Far better, they thought, to bottle it up and never mention it. In an era when manly courage was seen as a badge of honour, they chose to fight a silent battle rather than show any sign of weakness.

Researchers have long pondered the likelihood of veterans of the Civil War and other conflicts suffering psychological trauma. They have weighed what we know now against the details from dusty old documents and ancient tablets. Making a definitive scientific case about something that happened hundreds or thousands of years ago is of course impossible. To the layman, though, it appears undeniable. In fact, one conclusion from all of these histories is glaring – it would be more remarkable if soldiers exposed to some of the worst horrors known to humanity had NOT suffered terrible mental scars as a result.

It was World War One that brought arguably the greatest leap forward in understanding. The Great War revolutionised medicine as doctors responded to death and injury to an extent never before seen. The mechanisation of armies had brought killing and maiming on an industrial scale. At the cost of millions of lives, came advances in orthopaedics, treatment for burns and facial injuries, the development of prosthetics and vaccinations and antiseptics. Systems for treating the wounded on the battlefield improved, new hospitals were built, healthcare systems became more organised. Doctors also had to confront an army of men with injuries no one could see.

The years between the end of the Civil War in 1865 and the start of World War One in 1914 had seen PTS-like symptoms described and diagnosed in a variety of ways. At a time when the likes of Sigmund Freud were awakening people to secrets deep in the mind, more and more psychologists and neurologists were beginning to probe the complexities and impacts of trauma. Freud described it as 'an experience which within a short period of time presents the mind with an increase of stimulus too powerful to be dealt with or worked off in the normal way'. With psychoanalysis, he was seeking an effective treatment for patients displaying what were called hysterical symptoms.

Numerous descriptions came and went. In France, they talked of 'traumatic neurosis' or 'traumatic hysteria'. In America, 'neurasthenia', a nervous exhaustion, was introduced. In Russia, they even had 'compensation neurosis', so-called because of new laws passed to compensate victims of those railway accidents. The German neurologist Hermann Oppenheim's adoption of 'traumatic neurosis' in 1889 had been controversial for blaming physical injury in the brain but it did lead to the use of the word 'trauma' in psychiatry for the first time.

Even as the 20th century dawned, soldiers who suffered PTS-like symptoms while fighting in the Boer War in South Africa were still being diagnosed with 'disorderly action of the heart'. Headaches and muscle paralysis were laid at the door of rheumatism and even 'railway spine' made a reappearance. The official report into the health of Boer War troops in 1904 concluded that carrying heavy weights on long marches was responsible and that previous sufferers of 'disorderly action of the heart' were prone to relapses because of the 'excitement or nervousness of going under fire'.

Ten years after that official report was released, millions of Europeans were facing a war on an altogether different scale. Within two months of Britain entering World War One in 1914, the first cases of soldiers suffering 'nervous and mental shock' began arriving back in England. At first, their symptoms were dismissed in the medical press as the rare, odd example of the strange things that can happen in war. But as the conflict escalated, the numbers grew. In December 1914, the *British Medical Journal* published a report from the consultant physician to the British Army in France. T.R. Elliott was surprised by the number of 'functional paralyses' being suffered by soldiers exposed to shell explosions but showing no signs of physical injuries. The men would become blind or deaf, unable to speak, seized by a violent tremor, their bodies shaking for days or completely paralysed. It was difficult to tell whether they may have suffered physical damage to the brain, he accepted, but he saw enough to concern him.

That winter saw the birth of a new term for what soldiers were suffering. The doctors, who until then had talked of functional disorders, hysteria and neurosis, soon adopted the phrase that soldiers themselves were using on the battlefield. They called it 'shell shock'.

The phrase appeared in an article in the medical journal *The Lancet* in February 1915. The psychologist Charles Myers, who had been commissioned into the Royal Army Medical Corps, wrote his account, 'A Contribution to the Study of Shell Shock, Being an Account of Three Cases of Loss of Memory, Vision and Smell', based on what he had seen at a hospital in France. 'Shell shock' would remain a popular term in the first half of the war but, on Myers's recommendation, was restricted in later years. Instead doctors were instructed to classify suspected cases as 'functional disorders' that were 'Not Yet Diagnosed (Nervous)'.

In those first few months of the British involvement in the war, soldiers reported suffering amnesia, headaches, tremors and sensitivity to noise. It was reported that as many as ten per cent of British officers and four per cent of regular soldiers were suffering from nervous and mental shock.

At the time, the National Hospital for the Paralysed and Epileptic in Queen's Square in London was the world's leading centre for the treatment of neurological disorders. The 462 soldiers who were admitted to the hospital suffering from functional disorders between 1914 and 1919 gave doctors perhaps the clearest insight ever into the impacts of combat on the mind. In a study of World War One case records from the hospital, Stefanie Linden and Edgar Jones wrote: 'As the war unfolded the number of physicians who believed that shell shock was primarily an organic disorder fell as research failed to find a pathological basis for its symptoms.'

It is estimated that some 80,000 patients were admitted to hospital in Britain suffering from 'shell shock'. Germany reported 600,000 'war neurotics', and more than 1,600 Australians would be diagnosed. The scale of the problem in Britain was apparent early on in a newspaper appeal from Lord Knutsford: 'If not cured, these men will drift back to the world as wrecks, and miserable wrecks, for the rest of their lives.'

The noise of modern warfare, the close-quarters combat, the sheer extent of the death and injury around them and the relentless nature of the war was literally driving men mad.

Case notes for an 18-year-old private from the London Scottish Regiment reveal the horror of the trenches: chronic thirst, heavy rain, poor diet, eye strain. The responsibility to handle the dead and wounded: 'The first day he was in a trench he had in his line of vision a pile of corpses one of which had the face turned towards him and appeared to be sleeping – this made such an impression on him that he cannot free himself from this vision.' The noise and fear of shells caused unease and strain. His comrades reported he didn't answer when they spoke to him, he was unable to shoot properly, he was shaky and suffered from headaches.

With massage and aspirin, the doctors reported 'a considerable improvement' was achieved.

More evidence that soldiers with 'shell shock' could be cured exists in the numerous films made by hospitals at the time. In one, recorded at the Royal Victoria Hospital in Netley in Hampshire, a Private Read, who had been buried by a shell in August 1917, is seen with his 'hysterical gait', swaying movement and with a 'nose-wiping' tic. After treatment and re-education, the tic had disappeared and he is shown walking and even running almost normally. A month later we see him feeding the animals on the farm at the Seale Hayne Military Hospital in Devon. The films were groundbreaking in revealing the work of doctors with shell-shocked patients. But they also exposed a reality of what life in the trenches could do to men beyond what were traditionally thought of as war wounds.

If modern medicine held out some hope, there is no doubt that those who were cured were the lucky few.

At the National Hospital, doctors noticed that a number of those suffering 'shell shock' had never actually been exposed to combat. Records from German doctors found the same – just the anticipation of danger could trigger the same reactions as any actual threat. The picture was becoming increasingly clear that the physical explanation for 'shell shock' was not sustainable. By the end of the war, doctors in Britain believed that psychological factors lay at the heart of 'shell shock'.

Still there were those who accused sufferers of being 'malingerers' or cowards, men too weak-willed to fight. We will never know how many of the more than 300 British and Commonwealth soldiers who were 'shot at dawn' for desertion, disobedience, mutiny or cowardice were, in reality, suffering the crippling psychological effects of combat. Some 700 Australian World War One soldiers were convicted of injuring themselves to escape battle. The official pardons for those who were executed – finally removing the shame and placing their names on the war memorials alongside their comrades – were only to come 90 years later.

And whatever the advances in medical knowledge, many military officials remained dubious about 'shell shock' for years.

Thomas Dowell was 25 when he enlisted in the Australian Army's 14th Battalion in Melbourne in 1914. In the ill-fated campaign at Gallipoli, he had spent four months in the firing line, facing shelling and bayonetting, surrounded by the dead and wounded of his own side. In August 1915 he was taken prisoner by the Turkish. He was held for three and a half years, suffering near starvation, threats of brutal violence and emotional torture. His captors performed numerous surgeries on his injured leg, most without anaesthetic, and loudly pondered its amputation. His descriptions of that time in captivity are graphic and horrifying. Before enlisting, he told his commanders he had been 'in perfect health, bodily and mentally' with no hint of any nervous condition. Since his return, he said, he was a nervous wreck.

His wife Bessie's letters are full of the darkness. Two days after his return, she realised 'he carried the effects of war with him when he made known his intent to buy a gun and shoot a relative'. Episodes of paranoia and 'moods' would come and go. One night, on their small dairy farm in Mooroopna north of Melbourne, he climbed on to the roof and began firing his gun. 'He has had his sister on her knees begging him not to shoot her intended husband.' Time and again, Bessie says, when she noticed the mood descending, she resorted to hiding his gun among the bamboo on their lonely farm. The impulse to kill would come suddenly in a man who had withdrawn from his family. Their doctor told Bessie that her husband was a 'severely war-strained man'. In her writings, her desperate attempts to 'make life as cheerful as possible' while 'dreading at all times a return of the trouble' reek of sadness.

Chapter 8

Today her letters are heartbreaking to read. 'I have left the home on three occasions due to the fear for my children, he telling me that he would bomb the place, knowing how to make them, all one morning he spent doing this. He has lain down in the out-house with a gun beside him for several hours and walks about during the night, frequently upsetting us by packing up all the furniture.'

'He is a happy man but it seems to me to be unnatural. For years I have tried to hide the fact from strangers, friends would not become very much acquainted due to his strangeness and he has persistently refused to visit anyone, so to save trouble, I have kept to myself.'

Bessie Dowell's letters were written in support of her husband's claims for treatment for his 'nervous irritability'. She wrote despite his warnings to her not to contact the authorities. If she did, he told her, she 'would need an undertaker and a sheet'.

The files in the National Archives of Australia contain the official response. 'There is no evidence to connect any mental condition with war service,' writes the doctor assessing their case.

The couple – often living apart because of Bessie's fears for the safety of herself and her children – continue to argue their case. The military authorities continue to resist: 'Nervous irritability (Psycho-neurosis): declined'.

The doctors who examined this 'small nervous man' all agree that he suffered from nervous irritability but it took them years to accept that it was his war service, the ferocious fighting at Gallipoli and three and a half years in enemy custody that was responsible. During that time Bessie's pleas that this 'alarming and distressing' state of health was 'leaving a trail of disorder and

147

confusion' fell on deaf ears. 'It seems the wife's statement,' wrote one senior medical officer, 'was grossly exaggerated, therefore it is probable that other statements are.'

The life story of Thomas Dowell unfolds in page after page of medical notes, quarrels with the military medical authorities, prescriptions for various ailments, a man wracked with the physical and mental pain of an awful war. The file ends abruptly. The word 'deceased' in red ink across the front page, the military responsibility for Thomas Dowell, by then divorced from Bessie, signed off as discharged with his death in August 1946.

By then, of course, Australia and the world had been through another global conflict and had learned new lessons about the true costs of war. But World War One and the ravages of 'shell shock' have remained fixed in our consciousness as a period of a particular suffering which was largely misunderstood. In her book *Broken Nation* the historian Joan Beaumont writes that Australia had 'limited capacity to deal with the many thousands of men with psychological trauma. There were no trained psychoanalysts in 1914, and few medical practitioners familiar with Freudian theory.' By the 1930s, she writes, there were nearly 13,000 returned servicemen receiving pensions on psychological grounds.

The official figures show that World War One was the costliest in terms of death and injury that Australia ever fought. From a country of fewer than five million people, 416,000 enlisted. More than 60,000 lost their lives. But another 60,000 died between 1919 and 1929. For Sir Angus Houston, former Chief of Defence Forces and a patron of Stand Tall, those figures tell a story in themselves: 'I would submit that a lot were due to mental health issues from the war because suicide went unrecorded in that period.'

The history of PTS-like symptoms portrays World War Two as being more enlightened than previous conflicts. What had become known as 'combat stress reaction', battle weariness and exhaustion, has always attracted less attention than 'shell shock'. Perhaps this is due to the perception of World War Two as a more just war, perhaps because there was a greater effort to quickly identify and treat casualties of combat stress. Not everyone bought into it. One of America's most celebrated generals, George Patton, almost saw his military career prematurely ended when he berated and slapped two soldiers who were being treated for battle fatigue during the Allied campaign in Sicily.

Patton labelled one a weakling and the other a 'goddamned coward' before ranting that it made his blood boil to see 'yellow-bellied bastards being babied'. The medical staff were apoplectic. The investigation ordered by Dwight Eisenhower, commander of the Allied forces, ended with Patton grudgingly apologising. What was notable was that public and press opinion largely condemned Patton for his behaviour. One shocking revelation about the treatment of US veterans of World War Two would emerge decades later. Almost 2,000 lobotomies were performed on veterans demonstrating signs of mental illness between April 1947 and September 1950. It was a brutal last resort when other treatments failed and in the days before PTS was a recognised disorder.

The wars of the 20th century trace the development of understanding of combat stress, sometimes through the lines of one family. John George, who was a young lieutenant when he met Tony Dell in Vietnam, himself suffered the ghosts of that war when he came home. His father was at Gallipoli, enlisting at 17 years old. 'Number 642 to join up,' his son proudly says, but of what he experienced: 'Dad never spoke about the war.'

Through hundreds of years of warfare, from the battlefields in ancient Mesopotamia to the trenches of Europe and the paddies of Vietnam, soldiers faced experiences outside of the realm of normal human emotions. In the 1970s, finally progress was made in placing those experiences into context and ways were found for them to at least live with their scars.

Veterans of Vietnam like Tony Dell have reason to thank another young man, who was also pitched into that war, for realising that they would all need help if they were ever to live normal lives again.

9

AS TONY Dell basked in the glory of his first Test appearance for Australia, 10,000 miles away another young serviceman from the Vietnam War was coming to a realisation that would change both of their lives.

In April 1971, veterans of the war set up camp in the heart of Washington DC in the largest ever anti-war protest staged by those who had actually fought in it. It took place in open defiance of court orders which outlawed sleeping on the National Mall. It was entirely peaceful and the veterans, assembled by a group called Vietnam Veterans Against the War, took their message directly to the institutions of the US government. On the last day of the week-long protest, more than 800 veterans, dressed in battle fatigues, threw their medals, ribbons and discharge papers on to the steps of the Capitol.

One of those who took part was Charles Figley. He had joined the US Marines straight out of high school and was in Vietnam as the war began to escalate in 1965. It had felt like a thrilling adventure for a young man from America's Midwest. But Figley soon realised it was nothing but a fight for survival. By the time of the protest he was studying human development at university. He decided he had to join his fellow veterans in Washington.

Figley says he was struck by how many of them were suffering. He saw relationship problems, substance abuse, anger issues. It was hard to miss, sleeping out among them on that impromptu campsite on the Mall: 'I could hear them screaming at night.' He suddenly felt a responsibility to help. He started to record what he was seeing, the veterans were 'walking audio-visual aids for how war can affect you'. The following year he started a clinical support group for veterans who were studying at a university in Ohio, and still struggling with their memories of the war. Charles Figley was to write the first book ever published on PTS-like symptoms.

Stress Disorder Among Vietnam Veterans came out in 1978. It detailed the impact of combat-related trauma and the real potential for long-term consequences. It also offered advice to doctors on how to help sufferers. Figley had reached back into history to draw inspiration from the reports of so-called hysterical reactions collected by an ancient Egyptian doctor. The *Kunyus Papyrus*, published in 1900 BC, is regarded as one of the first medical texts and it contained some striking parallels with the Vietnam generation. For Figley, it also served as a warning. 'It was clear that this had been around for a long time. This was part of living and a fundamental part of the human experience. We had not addressed the problems – for those in combat there was just a "good luck" when they left.'

Charles Figley was one of a band of researchers who had begun exploring the field of post-traumatic stress in the mid-70s. The decision of the American Psychological Association to include PTS in its manual in 1980 was a direct consequence of their work.

It had an immediate impact. Millions in government money was freed up to train professionals to work with Vietnam veterans and provide community support centres. There was also a recognition at last of the need for specialist healthcare services.

One other side benefit for veterans came in America's courtrooms. Those suffering PTS could now point to combat trauma in their defence case. An earlier legal term, 'traumatic war neurosis', had been summarily removed from the law guidelines in the early 1970s, catching defendants and lawyers unawares.

There is some irony that the official recognition of PTS was born out of the heat of those anti-war protests. The sheer unpopularity of the Vietnam War had caused many veterans, Tony Dell included, to feel unable to talk about their experiences and emotions when they returned home. 'Not one person in my family asked me a question or mentioned where I had been for 12 months,' he said. By bottling it up, they undoubtedly made things worse. Figley told audiences that veterans felt guilt for the killing they carried out and neglected by the people they were supposedly fighting for back home. Change only started to come when society confronted what had happened to those young soldiers, even if it was in a war that many abhorred.

Tony Dell had returned home in 1968 to a country that was changing. The first thing he noticed were not the anti-war protests: it was the mini-skirts. 'I couldn't believe them.' Everything felt different from the country he had left a year before. It felt like time had stood still for him. While he had seen nothing but green jungle and army fatigues for months on end, psychedelia had arrived on home shores.

He stayed for a few days in Sydney. It was there he heard the music of Jimi Hendrix for the first time. He had never followed the example of many a soldier serving in Vietnam and experimented with drugs. But back home, hypnotised by the strobing lights at a party, his brothers passed him his first joint. It was a disconcerting time. 'I was restless. I felt like a fish out of water.'

As he hit the road from Sydney back to Brisbane in his mother's old green Falcon – earning a speeding ticket on the way to welcome him home – the change in the tone of the Australian public's view of the war was evident.

The largely peaceful sit-down protests involving a few hundred demonstrators in 1965 had given way to full-scale riots by 1968. Police and protestors fought a 'savage street battle' in Melbourne in July. For the first time in 25 years, mounted police were deployed to the streets, horses charging the crowds to bring order. Protestors armed with bottles, rocks and razors tried to storm the police station. Both sides emerged bloodied and bruised. The anti-war mood was gaining intensity and the protests were becoming more organised. Country-wide moratorium marches, modelled on those that had taken place in the United States, began in May 1970. Australians were encouraged to 'stop work to stop the war'. In Melbourne, 100,000 people turned up on a Friday afternoon to show their support, stunning the organisers and authorities alike. Further marches took place in September and June of the following year, the latter focused on encouraging young Australians to avoid the draft.

Chapter 9

The mothers of drafted soldiers in the 'Save Our Sons' campaigns were committed enough to accept arrest outside National Service induction centres.

Just as in America, the Australian view of the war in Vietnam was a complex one.

It had been in the twilight of a chilly October evening in 1966 that Air Force One touched down at Canberra Airport, bringing a sitting American president – and his bed – to Australian soil for the first time. Lyndon Johnson stopped off en route to a summit in Manila which was aimed at straightening out the aims and objectives in Vietnam.

In Australia, Johnson knew public feeling was growing against involvement in the war. This was to be a charm offensive. Greeted on the tarmac by Prime Minister Harold Holt, Johnson gave the crowd a tribute to the 'cream and flower of your young manhood who have rendered such gallant and distinguished service in Vietnam'.

Four months earlier, during a ceremonial address on the South Lawn of the White House, Holt had cribbed Johnson's campaign slogan and declared that Australia was 'all the way with LBJ'. It went down badly at home, appearing sycophantic to many. One parliamentarian said Holt's words 'shocked and insulted many Australians, its seeming servility was an embarrassment and a worry'.

It also emboldened the growing anti-war movement in Australia. No one had forgotten by the time Johnson landed in Canberra.

Holt had only taken office ten months earlier and was a confirmed cheerleader for Australian involvement alongside the

US in Vietnam. 'Unless there is security for all small nations,' he said in his first policy speech as prime minister, 'there cannot be security for any small nation.' Australia, he said, was 'paying a price for the freedoms we hope to retain'.

Holt and Johnson were old friends. They had known each other during World War Two, when the future American president was a young naval officer serving in Melbourne.

His reception in 1966 was rapturous. Half a million people turned out to greet him in both Melbourne and Sydney. But the cheering crowds and ticker-tape parades could not disguise an edge of dissent. Some felt it smacked of subservience, 'the shoe-licking nature of the Australian government', wrote Chris Topp of the Australian National University.

The red carpet reception was not universal. LBJ's presidential limousine was pelted with paint bombs by anti-war protestors as his motorcade ride through Melbourne took on a slightly chaotic air. A lawyer for the arrested protestors wrote an apology to Johnson, claiming they had been 'excited to fever pitch' by his presence and carried away by the 'consequent air of exaltation and triumph'. A short-sleeved white shirt worn by one of the president's Secret Service detail, still bearing the faint decades-old green paint splotches, remains in the Museums Victoria Collection.

The protests during Johnson's visit were actually modest. The main event was a speech at Parliament House. In a hall overflowing with yellow bouquets, Johnson departed from his prepared remarks to make what appeared to be a direct plea for continued support from the Australian people. Punctuating his words with short, sharp claps, he told the hall: 'There's not a boy that wears the uniform yonder today that hasn't always known that when freedom is at stake and honourable men stand in battle shoulder to shoulder, that Australians will go all the way, as Americans will go all the way.' Like a country preacher, he raised his hands and implored them: 'Not a third of the way, not part of the way, not three-fourths of the way, but all the way until liberty and freedom have been won.'

The following words came to define his visit: 'I'd like every Aussie standing in the rice paddies to know that every American and LBJ are with Australia all the way.'

Tony Dell was a few months away from taking his turn in those rice paddies. Whatever young Australians made of Johnson's words, the anti-war sentiment was only to grow. The president would leave office just over two years later, having decided to not seek re-election, disillusioned and defeated by the costs and confounding complexities of the conflict in south-east Asia.

Prime Minister Holt's perceived faux pas in Washington ultimately did little damage to his political reputation. Less than a month after Johnson's visit, he won by a landslide in the federal elections, his first and only election as prime minister. In December 1967, he parked his maroon Pontiac at a Melbourne beach he knew 'like the back of his hand' and dived in to the ocean. He was never seen again. Johnson was among the world leaders to attend his memorial service.

At the time of Holt's death, Tony Dell had been in Vietnam for seven months. One of the more than 49,000 Australians to see action there, the cost to him and many of his comrades would be personal and long-lasting.

If Dell was unaware of that impact in those early days, there were many men, like those who had camped out alongside Charles Figley, who knew things were not right. They came home and found society unprepared, and maybe unwilling, to confront what the veterans of the war needed. They felt abandoned and they faced the same choice as millions who had gone before them: suffer in silence or own up to mental struggles. In those less-enlightened times, taking the second option, they knew, came with huge risks attached. It meant that some of the cries for help were desperate.

The sound of gunfire had shattered the peace of a cool summer's evening. Thirty residents, pulled away from watching the evening news, reached for their telephones and called the police: a man was firing at passing cars, they reported. Within minutes, a swarm of officers was there, armed with high-powered rifles. They located the suspect on a building site for a new apartment complex. Cornered, he yelled at them: 'I've got you covered, sheriff – make a move and I'll kill you.' He fired three times before he was subdued and taken into custody.

The gunman arrested that night in Los Angeles in 1965, armed with a stolen revolver, was 24-year-old Harry Brannam. He had been discharged from the US Army four months earlier. For some of his six years of service he had been in Vietnam. His mother told reporters her son had been suffering 'battle fatigue'. He was haunted by the faces of Viet Cong guerrillas killed by his unit. She showed police a letter from his commanding officer confirming his story. The flashbacks were not what had tipped Harry Brannam over the edge, though. His local veterans' hospital, his mother said, had refused to treat him

Chapter 9

because he was not a veteran of World War One or Two or the Korean War.

Harry Brannam was not the first and would certainly not be the last soldier to hear the message when he came home from Vietnam. From the early days of the war, both in the United States and allied Australia, veterans were getting used to being told that the place where they had seen service was 'not a real war'.

Brannam's story and the reaction to it – one newspaper covered it under the headline 'Crazed Viet Vet Guns Cars' – was an early taste for the public of the psychological cost of their new war and how those coming home were feeling vulnerable and ignored. Hollywood would do much to perpetuate the image of the damaged Vietnam veteran in the years to come but for the veterans and those close to them this was real life in all of its extremes.

Tony Dell certainly remembers that phrase 'not a real war' and so do many of the mates he served with. With hindsight we can see the cause and effect. Because they were made to feel ashamed of *their* war, they stayed silent. In the silence, the trauma festered away for years.

Who could blame the Australian public when even some of their politicians were downplaying the significance of Vietnam? Senator J.P. Ormonde used a budget debate to slam 'the silly little war' being fought in Vietnam. 'It is not a real war,' he said. 'Why, even our soldiers have sent appeals asking what they are fighting for. Nobody wants this war.' A discussion about whether it was Australia's responsibility to protect Asia from communism was certainly a legitimate one. The language, though, served to fuel an environment in which it was easy to belittle the contribution of thousands of their own troops.

Twenty years later, Ruth Perkins was one of those with the job of unpicking the damage. She worked as a counsellor at a Vietnam veterans' centre and had spent three years listening to the stories. She told Melbourne's *The Age* that many veterans felt unable to talk about the war because it had become an irrelevance to society. 'If you had sacrificed two years of your life, not gone to university, felt great about wearing the uniform and then, when you returned, people said: "It wasn't a real war" or "You lost it, didn't you?" how would you feel? They had a pride in what they did. Now people say: "Why did you kill all those people?"'

What was an incredible part of their lives, she said, had to be shut down. 'The bad times fester, they have to keep a lid on it.'

Much of the blame was laid at the door of the Returned Services League. The RSL had been formed in 1916 to offer support to soldiers and sailors returning from World War One. By the time of Vietnam, the RSL was overwhelmingly run by those who had seen action in World War Two. Whether it was real or perceived, Vietnam veterans found the RSL an unwelcoming environment. Many say they heard that slur about *their* war not being a real one, either directly or second-hand, and it was enough to keep them away from the RSL. Vietnam veteran Les Blok told reporters in the 1990s: 'The RSL said, "Come back when you've been to a real war," which really turned us right off.' Ruth Perkins said: 'Veterans from every war believe their war was special. Vietnam veterans didn't feel there was an open acceptance and support for them by the RSL.'

'A very young Pom', Dell at home in England in the 1950s

Dell at high school in Cardiff in 1958

A soldier's life in Vietnam, in the camp at Nui Dat

A cricketer at war, Dell in Vietnam

'Armed and dangerous', Dell
in Vietnam

The soldier's morning routine in Vietnam

Private Dell, radio operator, in Vietnam

Private Dell at the 'horseshoe' command post in Vietnam

New boy Dell aims to give 'em hell

QUEENSLAND'S latest Sheffield Shield quickie, Tony Dell, has renewed a very lethal opening bowler partnership.

He has teamed - up with experienced Ross Duncan who was Tony's team - mate in Brisbane club cricket. Ross now is in Rockhampton and Tony has continued bowling for Easts.

Between the two of them, Tony's left arm thunderbolts and Ross's right arm swingers, they knocked over numerous

News of Dell's call-up to the Queensland side in 1970

The Queensland line-up including Dell for 1970/71 season

Queensland's new fast bowler in the nets in 1970

AUSTRALIA SHOULD RING BELL FOR TONY DELL

By BARRY RICHARDS as told to GEOFF KINGSTON

After watching Australia's innocuous pace attack being carved up again by the English openers it is difficult to imagine Australia winning another game in this series.

Alan Thomson bowled   he is able to bounce the
well and Dennis Liller in

he ruled that Geoff Boycott was run out.

The other 50 p.c. would have reckoned he was wrong.

I was probably in the worst position in the

been young boys who would have been impressed by what Boycott did.

They might think that if a great player like Boycott can throw his bat

The batting great Barry Richards gives Dell his blessing

GUM-CHEWING, SMILING TONY IS OUR TEST HOPE

TONY DELL, 23, bachelor, not even engaged, realises it well-and-truly now; but it took a while to accept that he was soon to play Test cricket.

Yesterday he was selected to play in the Seventh Test against England in Sydney next week. The news stunned both fast bowler Dell and the cricket world.

This is his first season in first-class cricket.

"I admit it," he said at the nets at Bottomley Park yesterday afternoon. "It knocked me completely sideways."

But, realistically Tony wasted no time — he hurried out to practice at the nets at 4 p.m.

What impresses people about Tony Dell, of course, is his height — six feet 4¼ inches, and well-proportioned with it at a neat 16 stone.

His shock of dark curly hair is not hippie-length — just carefree.

And his amiability. He does not push, but grinning easily, he co-operated when a cameraman asked him to perform against Sam Trimble yesterday. Nothing was too much trouble.

Dell lopes along always in top gear and he chews gum — again in a slow top-gear style.

Bowling, his shirt is out half the time — that's handy for wiping the ball.

Once he was a "Pommie"

He is English-born. At six he played cricket at primary school in Hampshire.

He came to Australia with his family when he was 12 and his father was sales manager in Brisbane for a big electrical-goods firm.

"Dad's a mad-keen cricket fan," Tony told me. "He just lives-cricket."

Did Tony phone Dad in Sydney to tell him about getting the selection? — "No," he grinned, "Dad phoned me."

He has a sister and two younger brothers. But, he says, they can take cricket or leave it, and usually they leave it.

His home life, his private life?

There isn't any really. He plays Rugby Union as second-row with Souths.

He reads when he has a chance. He lives in a flat at East Brisbane, but the flat does not see much of Tony Dell.

Tony went to "Churchie" (The Church of England Grammar School), and says it is the best cricket playing school in Queensland.

When his father took a job sales job in a Sydney international confectionery firm, Tony decided to stay in Brisbane.

He works for an advertising agency as its media manager.

"I'M THE BEST": LAWRY — Page 16

QUEENSLAND fast bowler Tony Dell who has been chosen in the Australian team for the seventh Test match, next Friday, cooking in his East Brisbane flat last night.

Call-up 'knocked me completely sideways':
Australia's new sporting sensation

GIANT PACEMAN IS A GAMBLE FOR TEST

By PHIL WILKINS

EACH earthquake has its own signature and just how deeply giant pace bowler Tony Dell imprints his name on the seventh Test should settle the Ashes argument.

Australia's selectors are not men inclined to betting on flies on the wall but during dinner at Sir Donald Bradman's Adelaide home on Wednesday night, there came a moment for a silent prayer and a gamble.

It was beyond all of them by sheer frustration.

The selectors have ransacked their lockers for genuinely fast bowlers to put against England this summer and until they found Dennis Lillee, it was a depressing pastime.

Graham McKenzie was the big tip to return to the team for the final Test, the only catch being a doubt about a back injury.

A Sheffield Shield match report from Neil Harvey probably influenced the three selectors to put their necks out and choose Dell.

Harvey was in Brisbane these weeks ago watching Queensland in action against probable Shield winners, South Australia.

What he saw of Dell — in only his eighth first-class game — he liked.

The left-arm opening bowler took 1-88 in the first innings and had several chances missed, and then 6-76 in the second innings.

He even had South Africa's Test batting champion Barry Richards backpedalling which caused Richards to write that Dell was the quickest bowler he had faced in Australia.

Quickest

"His first five or six overs are as good as I've seen, and his bumper can be frightening," Richards said.

"That recommendation was good enough for the selectors."

Dell, in his initial first class season for Queensland, went into the Australian Test side.

Had it not been for his father's employment posting to Brisbane when he was a 14-year-old schoolboy, Dell might have been playing for England next Friday.

He was born in the English county of Hampshire and as lad preferred Rugby Union to cricket

TONY DELL

In 1967 he went to Vietnam with 2 Battalion and was involved in the bloody Tet offensive.

"When things were quiet I used to listen to Radio Australia to the Shield broadcasts," he recalled.

"Peter Allan was retiring and Queensland were trying opening bowlers left, right and centre, to replace him, and once I was in the Army in Vietnam."

At the end of 1968 he was binding on his size 11½ cricket boots again for Queensland Colts and at the SCG No. 2, he took 4-71 from 30 overs in NSW Colts' first innings.

SGB Queensland's selectors were not convinced and he had to bund the Brisbane competition for two seasons before they talented and admitted him to the team.

Now 25, Dell has taken 20 wickets in his eight games at an average of 33 runs per wicket, having the left-hander's natural inswinger and slanting the ball to the slips to the right-handers.

Dell is a reserved young man, a dark-haired bachelor, employed as an advertising media manager, modest and assured.

"He amazes you," one of his Test colleagues said yesterday. "You think you're settling in nicely and then he makes one really fly."

Give curry

"He seems to hit the seam and it's up at your eyes. He'll give the Englishmen some curry."

Dell is a cumbersome fellow understandably, although his 14-stride approach is controlled, rarely flinging himself into his bowling as does Dennis Lillee.

"If I was wiry it would be different. If I threw myself around, I'd probably break my back," Dell says.

Dell knows all about the war zone. When the hot lead starts flying at the SCG on Friday, he could be grateful for the experience.

"It promises to be better than the gunfight at OK Corral."

Not everyone was convinced by Dell's
call-up

Dell's first Test wicket: John Edrich, caught by Greg Chappell, at SCG in February 1971

'I don't think we'll have much to fear': Ray Illingworth faces Dell at SCG in February 1971

The last days: Dell alongside Greg Chappell in Queensland squad in 1974

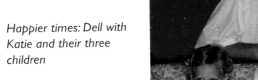

Dell quits the Shield scene

QUEENSLAND'S international fast bowler Tony Dell yesterday confirmed his retirement from first class cricket.

"I have rung State selector Ern Toovey

The end: Dell quits first-class cricket in 1975

Happier times: Dell with Katie and their three children

With the 'mum' of Stand Tall: Tony and Sally

Chapter 9

Tony Dell was one of those who stayed away. Kevin Alcock, the schoolfriend who ended up alongside him in Vietnam, remembers marching with his platoon in Brisbane one ANZAC Day parade when he saw Dell, with his son sitting on his shoulders, watching as they came past. 'He never marched,' Alcock remembers.

By the early 1980s, the Australian government had at last begun to recognise the problems affecting its Vietnam veterans. In 1982, ten years after the last of the country's troops had come home, a number of counselling centres were opened across the country. Two weeks after it opened, the first of them, in Frewville in Adelaide, was seeing ten people a day, some with serious and complex problems. One of the resident psychiatrists said the problems had been aggravated over the years and were often 'heightened by solitude'. John Warner added: 'The Vietnam veterans don't congregate, they've lost track of the mates they had overseas and a lot of them have become isolated.' Many, he said, had avoided affiliation with their local RSL and made no claims for a pension or treatment. That first decade back home for many was a desolate time for many veterans.

There is no doubt that the RSL and the Australian authorities did respond to the perception that Vietnam veterans were being treated differently. In 1972 the League decided that veterans who served in Vietnam should lead the annual ANZAC Day parade through Sydney. An estimated 150,000 attended and other events across the country also attracted large crowds. A 'Welcome Home' parade was held in Sydney in October 1987, almost 15 years after the last soldiers had actually come home. A crowd of 60,000 watched 25,000 veterans march in what Prime

Minister Bob Hawke called the 'recognition at last extended to our Vietnam veterans'. A Vietnam War memorial was finally unveiled in Canberra in 1992.

To this day though, many veterans feel a burning injustice about how they were treated in those early days. Kevin Alcock, who was himself later diagnosed with PTS and went on to serve on the committee of his local RSL branch, is one of many who talk of a young woman protestor throwing red paint at the battalion as they marched through Brisbane. The anger lives on too over the stories of trade union members refusing to load supply ships bound for the war effort in protest at Australia's involvement.

It is telling that these are the memories that persist for many Vietnam veterans. Researchers have identified only one 'red paint' protest ever having been reported towards marching soldiers. In June 1966, a 21-year-old typist called Nadine Jensen, wearing 'one of her best dresses', doused herself in a mixture of kerosene, turpentine and red paint, and threw her arms around the lieutenant colonel who was leading the homecoming march through Sydney. The red, she said, symbolised the blood being shed in Vietnam. The following day, her hair still caked with the remnants of the red paint, she was fined $6 for a charge of offensive behaviour. She told the court her protest was not aimed at the soldiers but at the higher authority that sent them to war and the complacency and apathy in the country. The presiding magistrate told her: 'I don't know whether I should remand you in custody and have you psychiatrically examined.' Jensen replied that she had been psychiatrically examined twice and the doctors told her there was nothing wrong with her.

Chapter 9

It remains possible that there were other Nadine Jensens, women or men who took their anti-war message out on marching soldiers in Australia, and whose exploits were not covered by newspapers at the time. But, in his book *The Vietnam Years*, the writer Michael Caulfield suggests there was widespread misremembering by veterans feeling hurt at the neglect they felt.

'Every Vietnam veteran I have talked with remembers the woman and the red paint, the perceived insult to their uniform, to their service. But not one of them spoke of the half a million people, or the enthusiasm of the reception. One single action, one potent photograph has become the accepted truth.'

In facts, reports from the time of that parade in Sydney tell of a joyful event of women kissing soldiers and telephone directories torn up to make confetti. The handful of activists who attempted to disrupt the events often got short shrift: one beaten by an elderly man with a walking stick and two others attacked by a woman with an umbrella.

But talk to many veterans and that is not the welcome they remember.

Caufield describes a mythology about the war that has grown as the years have passed. No, he writes, soldiers were not spat at, doused with blood or called 'baby killers.' They were not social misfits or loners, prone to alcoholism and violence. They were welcomed home and did receive public support. The bigger problem was that the Australian public was 'either ignorant or confused' about what their soldiers were doing in Vietnam and whether they succeeded or not.

Whatever the reasons, the stories that many men tell of their Vietnam have become their own personal legends, seasoned in the decades of telling, passed down to their children, and fuelled by a very genuine feeling that they were not treated as heroes.

They had seen their fathers' generation come back from World War Two to be honoured and feted by a grateful nation, eased on to the path of successful post-war lives. It had been seen as a just war, said Charles Figley, with entire nations on board; to be opposed to fighting it put you in the minority. Vietnam was different. It divided people. There was a culture clash about the rights and wrongs. How could the men caught in the middle of that feel like heroes?

Veteran Les Blok told the *Sydney Morning Herald* in 1994: 'I never told anyone I was a Vietnam veteran because of the way we were treated when we got back. The government treated us badly, the television was against us, the public seemed to be against us. It was the only war Australia fought in which we didn't bloody win and we didn't come back as heroes.'

That so many veterans returned showing the symptoms of post-traumatic stress further alienated them from society. The recognition of PTS as a condition undoubtedly helped veterans and civilians alike in their understanding. But those working in the field of veterans' mental health were also starting to see a variant in the post-war suffering of soldiers.

In the 1990s, a psychiatrist at a US Department of Veterans' Affairs clinic in Boston identified a different form of psychological trauma among veterans. Dr Jonathan Shay called it 'moral injury'. In effect, soldiers were suffering an injury to their conscience. In battle they had violated their core values or been exposed to such evil that their whole sense of right and wrong had been shaken. The act of killing civilians or doing something with no regard to whether it might take innocent lives would be unthinkable to them at any other time in their lives. Even witnessing or hearing about such horrors of war can be enough to leave scars. The memories of those things are impossible to erase and veterans carry a burden of guilt or shame. They are disgusted with themselves, outraged at what they have done and unable to forgive themselves for it. Dr Shay's book *Achilles in Vietnam*, comparing the psychological toll on Vietnam veterans with that of soldiers in Homer's *Iliad*, has become required reading on the subject of the individual, personal devastation of war.

Moral injury is different to PTS, experts say. While some of the symptoms, things like flashbacks, disturbed sleep and self-harm, are certainly similar, it is an existential uncertainty that marks out moral injury. PTS is based in fear, a response to the risk of danger or threat; moral injury grips the sufferer with intense guilt. This distinction is hugely important when it comes to offering treatments to sufferers.

It was the experiences of Vietnam veterans that informed the early work on moral injury. At that time, it focused on the failings of leaders on the battlefield, the sense that soldiers were being led astray by figures of authority. It was the experiences of those who served in Iraq and Afghanistan that led researchers to conclude that an individual's own morals were the decisive factor.

Whatever era and whichever war though, they told a common story. When they came home, they hung up the uniform but were unable to shake off the emotional baggage. They no longer felt like the same person who had gone to war and found it difficult to relate to friends and family. One Vietnam veteran told researchers that, while on compassionate leave to attend his grandfather's funeral in 1968, he had been verbally abused by a relative for the part he was playing in the war. It was that experience, not anything he had done in combat he said, that struck him to his core. The people he trusted the most had inflicted an unbearable trauma. This, he said, was the moment that began a long post-war journey into alcoholism.

Just like with PTS, not everyone who experiences a moral crisis in combat will end up with a moral injury. Not everyone who experiences a trauma suffers post-traumatic stress. But also, just like PTS, it is hard to imagine how anyone experiencing the horrors of war could not return with some level of emotional scarring.

Whether it was veterans like Tony Dell, who rarely spoke about their war and were never asked anyway, or those who tried but found society less than interested in listening, they all found a disconnect with the people on whose behalf they were fighting. Veterans felt the public could never be expected to really understand what they had experienced in Vietnam.

In the early 1980s, an American television documentary called *Vietnam Requiem* profiled five Vietnam War veterans who had been jailed for violent crimes since returning home. At the time, combat veterans were twice as likely to have been arrested than those of the same age who had not been to war. The greater the exposure to combat, a study had found, the more likely a veteran's chance of arrest or conviction. All five of those featured in the documentary had been commended for bravery in battle but had returned home to an ambivalent America. Their lives were consumed by addiction and violence.

Chapter 9

One of the most striking voices in the documentary is that of Albert 'Peewee' Dodds, a former sergeant who was then serving seven years for attempted armed robbery. His assessment of the war and its cost was stark.

'You're 18 years old and you're wearing somebody's brains around on your shirt because they got their head blown off and that's not supposed to affect you? I can never understand that. What would scare me is if we were to send a group of 18-year-olds 12,000 miles away and subject them to a year of that obscenity and have them NOT being affected. That's what would frighten me.'

A generation of young men, along with a relatively small group of women, were exposed to the horrors of the Vietnam War. Decades on it is impossible to calculate how many lives were blighted by the psychological impact.

Professor Charles Figley has had years to ponder how he was affected by his experiences of fighting in Vietnam. His research into the effects of combat stress, along with his campaigning and writing on the subject, undoubtedly helped him process thoughts and emotions that others suppressed. He also credits his volunteer work during his time in Vietnam, working with his old high school in Ohio to ferry education and hygiene supplies to a Catholic orphanage and school near his Marine unit in Da Nang. This service-as-therapy was a prelude to a life and career as an internationally renowned trauma expert. After bringing his expertise to the aftermath of Hurricane Katrina, he made New Orleans his home. He is in demand the world over for his knowledge of disaster-related trauma. But he was not immune from the effects of his time with the US Marines in Vietnam in 1965.

When he left the military two years later to return to civilian life, he remembered, it became his habit to never lock the doors when he was at home. It was only in recent years that he wondered why. When he forced himself to think about it, he realised he was still carrying a need to defend himself. The war-hardened Marine was daring an intruder to take him on. 'The need to do battle was still within me.'

Some carried this war within more successfully than others. The advances in understanding of post-traumatic stress have made a huge difference to the lives of many Vietnam veterans. Even if it took them some years to get there, there is some peace in the understanding. Some never got the chance to reach that place – the burden was too great.

10

THE REGAL Park Motor Inn in Adelaide felt much more sophisticated back then. The main staircase felt wider and grander, the lobby had an ambience of glamour. The modernist two-storey on Barton Terrace had only opened four years earlier, 'a welcome sight' for travellers, said an advertisement in the Australia travel magazine *Walkabout*, even if it did print the wrong address. In February 1973, the Queensland cricket team had found their way to the Regal Park, on the second stop of that season's southern tour in the Sheffield Shield. That week at the Regal Park would come to be a significant one in the sweep of Tony Dell's life.

Queensland's cricketers were not the only sporting competitors staying in the motel. The National Springboard and High Diving Championships were taking place a ten-minute walk across the park at Adelaide's Aquatic Centre. The team from Western Australia were holed up at the Regal Park too, among them a confident doctor's daughter from Perth. Sally Hodder had been having trouble with one of her dives. Kept back for extra practice one evening, she was freezing cold, running late and not looking where she was going as she charged up that main staircase at the Regal Park. She ran, literally, straight into a giant figure coming the other way. 'Who are you?' she demanded. 'I'm Tony Dell,' came the reply. 'Well, nice to meet you, now get out of my way.' Luckily for both that frosty first meeting between precocious young diver and gnarled cricketer would develop into something much friendlier.

It had been another miserable and frustrating season for Queensland and an overnight downpour in Adelaide had washed out the last day of the match with defeat looming against title-chasing South Australia. They also had to contend with a squabble with the diving team over the two clothes dryers in the laundry room back at the hotel. 'We had loads of towels so we would chuck their cricket creams out of the dryers so we could use them,' remembers Sally. 'There were constant, big fights in the drying room.'

They were getting hot and bothered all over Australia during that summer of 1973: sweltering humidity, talk of fuel strikes and tax rises and protests against the Vietnam War still flaring in the streets. That February, Adelaide, usually so hot and dry, was emerging from a record-setting heatwave, successive days of temperatures skirting near 40°. It was the perfect environment for the divers of Western Australia and the cricketers of Queensland to get to know each other around the hotel swimming pool. Sally Hodder and friends even arranged a séance to seek some spiritual answers as to who would win the diving titles over the coming days. When they decided to invite the cricket team, she was deputed to crawl on her hands and knees into their team dinner and deliver the note, tapping a surprised Dell on the leg from under the table. 'It was all just a big joke to us,' she said. 'We were having fun, we all got along well.'

While her fellow divers headed home to Perth, Sally stayed on in Adelaide to compete in the open national championships. A few days later at the city's airport she was standing captivated, like so many travellers were back then, by the artist Stan Ostoja-Kotkowski's giant laser-generated mural *Space Scape* when suddenly everything went dark. Two giant hands had come from behind her and covered her eyes. It was Tony Dell again. After some awkward small talk, he took Sally's phone number, promising to arrange some tickets to watch the cricket when Queensland arrived in Perth a few days later. She remained convinced that it was the mention of her two older sisters that sparked his interest. Ten days later, after a rare victory against Victoria in Melbourne, Dell and his team-mates arrived in Western Australia and, true to his word, he phoned the Hodder household.

Over the next three days, Sally, her dad Ern, and her sisters Jenny and Felicity, would sit and watch in the members' area of the famous old WACA ground. Dell would occasionally join them. 'I didn't know much about cricket and he would come and sit with us and teach me about the game. That was where I started to develop my love for the game,' Sally said. It was also the start of a friendship not only between Sally and Tony but between the Queensland team and the Hodder family. On the field, Queensland were beaten with a day to spare, Western Australia's win confirming them as Sheffield Shield winners for the second year in a row. To help drown their sorrows, the Hodders invited the Queensland players to a barbecue at the family's home overlooking the Swan River in Mosman Park. 'We all got on well, we were just really good friends.'

But the story of that summer can't be told without noting that Sally Hodder had not yet turned 15. Tony Dell, Test cricketer and successful businessman, was 27. Both say there was nothing romantic about their friendship – 'purely platonic' is how Dell would later refer to it – and certainly nothing untoward. By the end of February 1973, less than three weeks after they had met, Tony Dell was back at his desk in Brisbane, the cricket over for another season, and Sally Hodder was back at school.

They would write to each other over the course of the year that followed, letters that Sally Hodder has kept to this day. It was nearly a year after they had last seen each other that the Hodder phone rang. 'We're back,' Dell told her in January 1974 as Queensland landed in Perth to face Western Australia again. He had recently forced his way back into the Australian national team, playing his second Test match against New Zealand. Things were looking up for the team too, unbeaten all season and with new captain Greg Chappell on his way to scoring more runs than anyone that season. In fact, Chappell's absence for the match in Perth coincided with Queensland's first defeat of the season.

Once again, if they needed help to soothe the pain of defeat, the Hodder family was on hand. Ern Hodder had become a member at the WACA by now. A doctor by profession, he would eventually become an unofficial team physician to Western Australia, and once again he opened his home to the Queensland players. The annual barbecue for the visitors from Brisbane was by now a tradition. Dell would also come on his own for the family's big Wednesday night meal. 'We just clicked together,' Sally said. 'He would tell stories. Sometimes he and I would go out and have a hamburger together. I was very precocious.'

It was clear, however, that this could not last forever. Despite a successful season, after his second Test appearance a month earlier he had declared himself unavailable to the selectors. It was clear to him his desire to carry on playing cricket was fading; a tipping point was looming. 'He'd say, "I don't know if I'll be back again, I don't know if I'll keep playing." He had problems with his knee and his shoulder.' Again, after a few days in Perth, Dell was off home and he and Sally said goodbye.

The pattern of cross-country letters in the winter and the annual cricket visit in the summer would continue for just one more year. It was in December 1974 that Queensland came to Perth, drawing their Shield game thanks in large part to a Chappell innings that *Wisden* described as 'majestic', before flying home in time for Christmas. They returned in January for the semi-final of the Gillette Cup one-day competition. The Hodders had planned a victory party for the Queensland team and it went ahead despite them suffering a thumping defeat. 'They used to bring the Queensland Cricket Association flag with them to fly from the pavilion. At that party I nicked it. I don't know what I did with it, but I ended up keeping it,' said Sally.

By now she was 16 and her feelings for Dell were changing. 'By then I had developed a bit of a crush on him, my first crush, the first love of my life I used to call him. I don't think it was the same for him, although he was certainly very fond of me.'

Whatever feelings might have existed hardly mattered. Tony Dell flew home in January 1975 and immediately retired from first-class cricket. He and Sally would not set eyes on each other again for 40 years.

It was back home in Brisbane that year that Dell finally put an end to the complications in his love life. Reading one of his final letters to her, Sally remembers, 'Just out of the blue, a paragraph, "Oh, by the way, I got married yesterday." It was really strange.'

Even without Tony Dell in their lives, the Hodder family's place in the social life of Australian cricket and touring teams had by now become fixed. She remembered consoling the giant West Indian fast bowler Joel Garner, so tall he had to duck through the doorways at the family home, sitting on a set of stairs, knees up to his chin, sobbing at being away from his wife and newborn child. But from 1975 Sally's connection with Tony Dell was to fade as fast as the letter-writing petered out.

One incident from the time she spent with him has come to assume greater significance in hindsight. The couple went for a meal at a steak restaurant during one of Dell's visits to Perth. Sally, young and excited at the outing, jumped at the first table they were offered. As she went to sit down, Dell stopped. '"No," he said. He wanted a booth in the corner so he could have his back to the wall and look out. I thought it was very strange at the time; we had a perfectly nice table.' The story fits with something else that never featured in all of their conversations at the time. 'I don't remember that he mentioned Vietnam at all.'

Over the following decades, college, marriage, children and careers pushed the memories of those three summers further into the dim recesses. They may have stayed there had Sally's sister Jenny not been listening to the cricket on the radio in November 2015.

Chapter 10

That year's first Test between Australia and New Zealand in Brisbane had been chosen to commemorate the centenary of the Australian and New Zealand Army Corps. Just ahead of Remembrance Day and in the year marking the 100th anniversary of the fateful ANZAC landing at Gallipoli, members of the armed services from both countries took part in a pre-match ceremony. The cricketing rivalry between the nations had always played out to the background of the ANZAC legend, a bond forged in courage and sacrifice on the battlefield. As the only living Test cricketer to have seen action in a theatre of war, Tony Dell was invited to take part in the commemoration as a guest of honour. During the Sunday lunch interval, he was interviewed by ABC Grandstand commentator Jim Maxwell. He talked cricket and conflict, where his experiences had taken him in life and what he hoped Stand Tall could achieve. Sally Hodder received a phone call from her excited sister.

This blast from the past had little impact to begin with. It was only a couple of weeks later that she got hold of a recording of the interview. 'I listened to it and thought, "It is really great what you're doing."' By this time Sally's own life was in flux. A mother of two grown children, her marriage was on the road to separation and ultimate divorce. She had also never forgotten the fleeting moments with the visiting cricketer from her teenage years. She decided to email, to say hello and to offer what help she could to Stand Tall from her home way out west. Her email began: 'You probably won't remember me.' The reply came within five minutes: 'Actually I don't remember you.' It was not what Sally had expected: 'That was the first line of the email. It was a crushing moment. He really didn't remember me?' So, Sally started to tell the story of their three brief summers and Dell continued to draw a blank. His only memory, he has said since, was that of a girl's flashing smile, flickering in his mind at the mention of the Hodder family or Perth. If there was a lingering schoolgirl disappointment in this, Sally ploughed on, the pair emailing back and forth. Then Dell asked if they could speak on the phone. 'I was hesitant,' Sally said. 'I thought, "What are we doing here?" This was x million years ago, there is a 13-year age difference and I was in the middle of a horrible separation and subsequent divorce. Do I need any long-distance complications, or to be getting involved?'

But they did talk. 'We spent hours on the phone,' Dell said. 'We would just talk and talk and talk. She would say stuff and I would start to remember these things.' They decided it was time to meet again. Dell flew to Perth and the pair began to catch up on those intervening 40 years. What started as an offer to help with the work of Stand Tall blossomed into something much more personal. They decided on a holiday together in New Zealand. The commuting between her home in Perth and his 2,500 miles away in Brisbane was beginning to make little sense. At Dell's urging, Sally moved east – 'He's very persistent, never say die,' she said – and he moved out of the home he had been sharing with his daughters.

Dell is candid about the impact the relationship with Sally has had on his romantic life. For 20 years, he said, any thought of intimacy had been absent. Things have changed: 'I couldn't live without her.' In an email to his three children, he wrote: 'It is safe to say I'm a different person with a brand-new lease of life. You all have an allegiance to your mum and I understand

176

that but I have a depth of love for Sally which I have never experienced before.'

The arc of that friendship and the closeness of the relationship put Sally in a unique position to judge the impact of Vietnam and post-traumatic stress on Dell. When they first met, she saw nothing of the brooding character he felt he had become by then. 'He was always a gentle giant, he wouldn't say boo to a goose, he was just a lovely, lovely person.' She accepted she was an awestruck schoolgirl and he was an international sportsman, adopting an 'on-tour' persona, away from the stresses and strains of home life. 'I don't think PTS had started to have a huge impact on his life at that point.' Back then though, who knew what to look for? Those who had known him before Vietnam certainly saw more aggression on the cricket field, a team-mate more prone to lose his temper. But, just as Sally had had no idea of his time in combat, those he played with, including the Chappell brothers, were equally in the dark. She finds it hard to believe that the cricket community could be unaware that a promising fast bowler, who had been knocking on the door of a senior career, had gone to war and come back, and not been asked some questions. The answer lies in that enduring truth for many Vietnam veterans: he didn't talk about it. None of them did.

Sally found the Tony Dell of 2015 very different to the one she had known all those years before. 'When he came to Perth and I went to meet him at the hotel, it was the first time I had seen him since 1975 and I was very surprised at his physical condition.' The intervening years had taken their toll on already battered knee and shoulder joints and on his personality. 'My recollection is of one week over a number of years and it was all very exciting back then. He was lovely and gentle and fun, always telling stories.'

Life with him in later years was very different. 'It is very difficult living with someone with PTS. It is very unpredictable. He can lose his temper at the drop of a hat, at something most people would consider the most trifling of things, the sort of thing that would just not merit sweating about, he'll lose it.' Social norms go out of the window at times like that. She told the story of Dell being asked to move from a seat on a train by the person who had pre-booked it. 'He lost it, he was swearing and belligerent, and people recoil, rightly so because it is not rational behaviour. I found it very difficult because I feel the need to mediate and calm things down and try to prevent him from getting biffed.' Just as quickly as he goes crazy over something, the storm passes – to him it is over and forgotten. Not so for Sally. 'I can't forget what you did five seconds ago.' When the gardener trimmed a hedge he was trying to regrow at home in Brisbane, Dell first ranted at him and then went indoors and turned his anger on Sally. 'I had to leave the house, I couldn't hang about.'

None of this is helped by the fact that Dell went 40 years without a decent night's sleep. 'Travelling is a chore, he doesn't like airports and crowds, queues or confined spaces.' She has learned to knock on the walls as she makes her way along the hall leading to his home office. 'If I go in and he doesn't know I'm there, he hits the roof, he's so startled.' They are all textbook symptoms of PTS but that makes it no less difficult for those who live with them. 'You adjust. I love what he does with Stand Tall but there are times when I go off and do my own thing to have a break.'

Chapter 10

Working alongside the man she calls Ant brought its rewards. Dell paid tribute to Sally as the 'mum' of Stand Tall. He praised her passion for writing, crafting the charity's news articles, press releases, speeches, funding applications, building relationships to push expansion and helping organise the Lightning Bolt convoys. But even he admitted that her greatest achievement may have been the Herculean one of 'keeping our inspirational leader calm'. The appreciation was mutual. 'His drive is crazy, he is so passionate and so dedicated to what he believes in. He will do anything to raise awareness and understanding of PTS. He'll go on for as long as he's got the fight in him.'

In fact, she believed Stand Tall had taken the place of therapy in Dell's dealing with his own PTS. He was reluctant to see a doctor for any psychological or even physical problem. She had to pester him to get medical help for worsening shoulder problems, one of them probably already beyond repair, and to see a neurologist for a shake that developed in his hands. 'He goes reluctantly. He just doesn't believe in that sort of thing, it is just the way he is.'

He was also initially reluctant to put his own personal story at the heart of the Stand Tall mission. 'He never likes to put himself forward. It is only in the last few years that he has started to use his own story, his own lived experience, as any part of what Stand Tall is. Before that he didn't want his name as any part of it.' It was only at the urging of his mentor Sir Angus Houston that he became less recalcitrant and used his own profile, as the war vet who played Test cricket and endured the ups and downs of PTS, to get people to take notice. 'You're not just a regular Joe Blow who went to Vietnam and got PTS,' Sally told him.

All of the work with Stand Tall, though, did little to allow Sally much of a glimpse into Dell's experience in Vietnam. 'He doesn't talk much about it even now. Whether he genuinely doesn't remember or there's a bit of self-protection, I have to believe that he doesn't remember.' She does believe that the botched patrol and unexpected night-time encounter with the Viet Cong all those years ago was where his condition was born. 'They really thought they were goners and I'm sure that with most PTS there is a key incident or trauma that is the trigger. It had to be something that severe.'

Whether it was the passage of time or the memory-blocking powers of PTS, a lot was lost to Tony Dell. 'My recollection of those five matches in Perth has vanished along with most of my career and Vietnam and my memories of my time with Sally.' Even in writing about their story years later he pegged that final meeting as having taken place after the four-day match in December 1974 rather than after the one-day semi-final defeat a month later.

Those memories that did survive were fragmentary. His old Queensland team-mate John Maclean had kept in touch with the Hodder family and every so often over the years would drop their name into conversation. It would spark in Dell 'an unexplainable image of us that would flash into my mind'. Sally must have left a lasting impression on him, whatever tricks his memory has played since.

He tried over the years to fill in the blanks himself on what was happening back then. 'As Sally says now, "Jesus, you were a 6ft 5in Australian cricketer and you're a handsome bastard; I find it strange you didn't have women hanging off you right, left and centre." But I think I was always rather shy in that respect and I got myself into a situation while I was on tour and Sally was only a child and we just had a connection.'

There had been one moment during those 40 years of separation when there was just a chance they could have reconnected. In 1997, Dell's old team-mate Maclean, who had been a wicketkeeper good enough to play Test cricket for Australia and receive an MBE for services to the game, was visiting Perth and met up with Sally and her sister. During their conversation, Maclean suggested to Sally that she should write to Dell. He didn't mention what his old mate was going through, the mounting debts, increasingly desperate fight to keep his head above water and hold his family together, but Sally believes it was on his mind. She told herself there was no way she was going to revisit a schoolgirl crush but Maclean persisted – he said Dell would appreciate it. Still, it took Sally a while to sit down and write that letter. She received a reply, full of pleasantries and painting a picture of a happy, successful life – 'it was a "nice to hear from you, everything is rosy and fine" letter – a story she came to know was utter rubbish because everything was far from fine. They exchanged those letters and that was that, the moment had passed. More than a decade on, Dell had no recollection of receiving or sending either. He read them again, though. Sally kept all of their letters.

Her presence by his side energised him, putting renewed meaning into a life he felt was meandering before she appeared. The charity too benefitted from a new approach. 'Stand Tall has come on leaps and bounds since she got involved. She is a sounding board too. She says things I've never thought of and now they happen because of her.'

Some of those who have known Dell for the longest saw the change Sally brought to his life. Greg Delaney, the fellow 'lunatic' he met on the school bus as a teenager and with whom he terrorised the streets of Coorparoo, had seen Vietnam turn his old friend from a passive guy into an angry man. It took time but the roughest edges of that temper started to soften. 'It has gradually resolved itself over the years, especially with his relationship with Sally. I think it has been fantastic for him. He's starting to become the old Delly again.' Their work with Stand Tall, he said, helped Dell deal with his own PTS.

Ross Johnston, the school wicketkeeper who gave as good as he got when it came to banter with the big fast bowler, worried for his friend's welfare at times as his life started to unravel. Sally arrested the slide. 'She was a big plus in his life, she's been amazing. It's only since she came back into his life that he's taking a bit of pride in his personal presentation. That's been good for him. He now looks as if he cares for himself, not just for the charity.' Johnston even saw signs of something he never expected – he thought Dell was mellowing. Bruce Tanner, another veteran of the schoolboy party set in the 1960s, grew up to be the accountant who put Stand Tall on its financial feet. He said Sally's presence in making some sense of the chaos was critical to its continuing existence.

At the heart of their story, though, was a remarkable sequence of flukes and coincidences. Without any one of those serendipitous moments, Sally said, as with so many relationships, the course of history could have taken a very different route. 'I'm a believer in fate and karma. It was always meant to be. All of the connections were bizarre. If my sister had not been listening to the radio that day, if he hadn't been invited on to that radio special for the commemoration, even back to if I hadn't been having trouble with my two-and-a-half somersault in Adelaide, I wouldn't have been running late and run into him on the stairs. It is quite bizarre how it all happened.'

Forty-five years after that meeting on the hotel staircase, the couple made a return trip to Adelaide. The city's Fringe festival that year featured the play *Shell Shock*, a darkly comic story of a British soldier coming home from war, full of optimism about returning to civilian life but instead beset by the crippling realities of PTS. 'The script is funny and the main character is a sweet, simple guy who is slowly ground down by an affliction he doesn't really even realise he has,' wrote the reviewer for the *Adelaide Advertiser*. There could be no more apt piece of art for Tony Dell or any of the millions who suffered like him. The play was based on a semi-autobiographical novel by Iraq War veteran Neil Watkin, who had taken up writing as creative therapy after being diagnosed with PTS. The one-man stage version, starring Tim Marriott, was produced to raise awareness of armed forces charities and their work with mental health issues. Even its name, that favoured shorthand from World War One for the symptoms of PTS, is a reminder of how lessons have been learned in one major conflict, only to be forgotten by the next.

While they were in Adelaide, Sally and Tony went back to the Regal Park Motor Inn. They stood on that very same staircase. The carpet and décor may have changed but the spot was unmistakable, little changed from that day in 1973. The reality perhaps could never have lived up to the picture held in

Sally's memory but the romantic nostalgia of the moment was palpable all the same.

Their renewed relationship, now in their advancing years, has included each other's children and grandchildren. The ups and downs of family life, the frictions and the loyalties, the personality traits to get used to. 'If you do wrong by him he's very slow to forgive,' Sally said. 'If that involves doing something to hurt his kids, he's even less likely to forgive.'

The Tony Dell who 'never shed a tear' was real, but not to be mistaken for the soul of someone who did not feel very deeply. The death of his mother and the premature passing of his brothers John and Chris continued to have an impact on him.

For all the challenges of life with PTS and the charity that consumed their waking hours, Sally was glad that life turned out how it did. 'It's an adventure, I've learned some amazing things, met some amazing people and seen some amazing places.' One thing that has never changed? 'He's asked me to marry him about 50,000 times. It looks like he's never going to get the message that that will never happen.'

Their story is a testament to the fact that memory is a complex and shifting landscape. What we once remembered we can so easily forget. What we thought lost forever can be brought back to the surface by a word, an image, a smell. One of the marvels of the human mind is that it can bury the memories that cause us pain. It never fully buries them though.

For proof of that we can look to that life story that Tony Dell began writing for his children. Memories missing from the early versions do appear later on. Of the woman who he once told, 'Actually, I don't remember you,' the woman he described as the third love of his life, he wrote this: 'The most cruel thing I have ever done was to write to her and casually mention that I had got married.'

A few years later, he wrote, he was with his wife Katie on the Sydney to Manly ferry when he saw Sally. 'The second most cruel thing I've done was to ignore her.'

11

THE STATISTIC is staggering: 22 military veterans take their own life every single day in the United States. It is a figure that has become so well-known as to be burned into a nation's consciousness, an indictment of how society is failing its veterans.

In Australia, a country with 300 million fewer people than the US, still one veteran takes his or her life every day. 'In the last ten years we've lost more people to suicide than we've lost on the battlefield,' said Tony Dell.

Not every veteran who takes their own life is suffering with PTS, of course. The military community mirrors the civilian one in so many ways. All sorts of everyday pressures and triggers can drive people to a place where they can see no other way out. But it stands to reason that many of them – diagnosed or undiagnosed – will have been suffering with the effects of PTS.

The very fact we now have the data to paint this grim picture is perhaps an encouraging sign. Society is at least now literally counting the cost. We have never been more aware of what war can do to its participants and those caught in the crossfire. We have even come to recognise that PTS can afflict those who have never been anywhere near a battlefield.

The term itself is so widely known. A simple internet search for 'PTS' in 2019 returned millions of hits: lists of causes and symptoms, resources and support, calls for recognition and understanding. Spend any time trawling these hits and one would think there is a safety net for sufferers. News coverage keeps PTS in the public eye: reports of a new treatment, new levels of suffering, a new way of understanding. Sadly, all too often the stories report on someone who was unable to cope with their PTS, and the harmful consequences to themselves or those nearby. Look through the headlines, picked at random on one day: 'Study Finds PTS Symptoms Alleviated by Cannabis Use', 'Five Minute Injection May Offer Effective Option for PTS', 'Family says suspect in acid attack is veteran, suffered PTS'. These stories demonstrate just how much PTS has come to be part of the conversation. They also reveal the darkness, the hope and, sometimes, the oddly uplifting – 'Veterans with PTS help rehabilitate injured sea lions'.

Society has even become sensitive to the debate over what to call post-traumatic stress disorder. There is a school of thought that characterising it as a 'disorder' carries a stigma that often leaves the most vulnerable unwilling to seek help. It led to a push from mental health campaigners to encourage society to use the term PTS instead of PTSD, in the hope it will make sufferers feel more able to open up about their experiences. The website of former US president George W. Bush says 'PTS is an injury, it's not a disorder'. Tony Dell's charity is 'Stand Tall 4 PTS'.

All the discussion – and the work of numerous charities just like Dell's – has served to bring the condition more out into the open. Research in the US has shown that around seven per cent of the population will have PTS at some point in their lives. When those figures are broken down, ten per cent of women and four per cent of men will develop PTS. The greater prevalence among women is explained by the far greater risk of sexual assault, and subsequent PTS. Expand those figures out to the global population, even allowing for variations in different environments, cultures and classes, and it is fair to assume that there are hundreds of millions of sufferers around the world. PTS is far from abnormal.

For military veterans especially the condition has come out of the shadows. Modern wars in Iraq and Afghanistan have forced a new generation to confront the psychological toll of war. Thousands of young men and women are coming back from intense, complex, multi-year wars and bringing mental trauma with them. Like the veterans of World War One and Vietnam, their experiences are shining a light on the problem. But if society has clearly come a long way in its understanding of the hidden scars, some veterans have been left feeling just as exposed, vulnerable and abandoned as their counterparts in history. For all the research and information, all of the knowledge we have amassed, that statistic remains: 22 veterans a day in the US alone. Just because we know what it is, doesn't make us better at dealing with it. The suicides, the misery, the trail of destruction, keeps on happening.

David Finney loved the 20 years he spent in the Royal Australian Navy. But, as a young father, he knew he was struggling with the effects of PTS. He wrote candidly about it in a series of powerful blog posts. The deployments to war zones and plucking refugees to safety, young children who had lost their parents, drowned bodies floating in the sea, had left their mark. So too the loss of his baby son Kayne, as Finney held him in his arms and attempted resuscitation. He had come to view his service medals as reminders of what had been lost. 'I look at them as a sacrifice I made to my life, leaving my daughter at home with a young wife as I sailed over the horizon. Holding a machine gun one day then a newborn the next, the constant internal conflict that tells me to be a family man, but also ready to sail to the other side of the world at a moment's notice.'

At night was when his PTS would bedevil him: 'I started having nightmares again, about getting my head stomped on, being in a fire, losing Kayne, picking up dying refugees, being pinned next to an over-speeding engine fearing for my life, being in that room in Timor full of bullet holes, barbed wire and blood, dreaming of being on that base in Bougainville surrounded by armed guerrillas, dreaming of being on that wharf in Dili while the city burned.'

Some of those nightmares, he wrote, 'were so real I would wake up shaking, screaming, in a bed full of sweat or worse'.

For months he had been seeking help. When he tried to arrange an appointment with a psychiatrist, he was told there were none in his state taking new clients. The next available appointment was three months away, in another state. A few weeks later, at the age of 38, David Finney took his own life. This is not a story from a different time, when we understood less about PTS; this is a story that reached its tragic conclusion in February 2019.

Yet David Finney's death was not the end of his story. In the depths of her grief, his mother Julie-Ann decided his loss was not going to be in vain. 'He desperately wanted to stay alive, but David was failed by a broken system,' she wrote. Numerous chances to save her son had been missed: 'David was just one of too many veterans losing their battle with PTS. This failure has created a whole new war zone for our veterans, one they can't come home from.'

With those words, Julie-Ann Finney launched a campaign for a Royal Commission into the rate of suicide among military veterans. 'I don't want to be the mother that fights for a Royal Commission and I don't want to be the mother that lost her child,' she wrote. 'I will not stop until we see action by our government. I owe it not only to my amazing son, David, but to all veterans and their families.' Government agencies, she saw, wanted to help but were bogged down by protocol and procedures, paperwork piling up as lives continued to be lost. The ghosts of 'mothers and fathers, husbands and wives, brothers and sisters and families and friends', dating back to World War One, hung over her own call, like theirs, for official government action on what she called a national tragedy.

Even as her campaign was beginning to attract nationwide attention, the roll call of veteran suicides continued to grow. When she heard of the death of 34-year-old army veteran Bradley Carr, she told *The Advertiser* in Adelaide she felt defeated. Carr had spent years trying to cope with the demons left by his deployment to Afghanistan and had made numerous attempts to take his own life. It was on a visit to the Gold Coast in search of treatment that he was found dead in his hotel room. He died on ANZAC Day. It was a story, like that of her son, that pushed Julie-Ann Finney on. 'For a short moment I thought of giving up,' she told *The Advertiser.* 'That is, until once again, it occurred to me that if I don't fight, then at least once a week there will be another beautiful man or woman down, another family broken and another mother experiencing overwhelming grief. I cannot live with that and nor should any Australian.'

Tony Dell, for all his sympathy with the families of those who have died in this way, is characteristically blunt about the calls for a Royal Commission on veteran suicides. It 'would take years, undertaken by all the wrong people, meanwhile up to 15,000 will have committed suicide. It needs people at the coal face to make recommendations and they need to start now.'

The Australian authorities have at least been counting the number of veteran suicides. If that seems to be the bare minimum we should expect, not every nation has been quite so diligent. Australia, like the United States and Canada, has been way ahead of the UK in trying to put statistics alongside the anecdotal evidence. An official report in Australia in January 2018 concluded that, in the decade beginning in 2002, the suicide rate among male veterans was 14 per cent higher than the civilian population. In Canada, a study found that veterans were at a significantly higher risk of death by suicide. The age-adjusted suicide rate for male veterans was 40 per cent higher than among civilians; for female veterans it was an astounding 80 per cent. The US collates records of the death of every veteran. It found that the suicide rate had increased by 35 per cent between

2001, the year of the start of the war in Afghanistan, and 2016. A veteran was twice as likely to take his or her own life than someone who had not served.

In the UK, a country with more than 2.5 million military veterans, it took until July 2019 for the Ministry of Defence to even begin to consider a system to record suicides among ex-service personnel. It had taken a high-profile newspaper campaign and accusations that the government was turning a blind eye to the problem to force their hand. A study of deaths among veterans who had served between 2001 and 2014 was to be expanded to include more recent service personnel and would be updated, in effect, producing a real-time monitoring of suicides. For veterans' families it was welcome news, if years too late.

In 2012, according to the BBC's *Panorama* programme, more soldiers and veterans took their own lives than died fighting the Taliban in Afghanistan. Researchers had written to every coroner in the country to request the names of soldiers and veterans who had killed themselves. They also analysed news reports of inquests, in the absence of government figures for ex-service personnel. The programme told the story of Lance Sergeant Dan Collins. The Welsh Guardsman had joined the army at 16 and, in Helmand province in the summer of 2009, had been shot twice, blown up by a roadside bomb and seen his friend killed by his side. His mother said he told her: 'This place is hell on earth.' When he returned home it was clear to everyone that the war had come back with him. Diagnosed with PTS, he spent ten months in treatment before being told he was fit to return to active service. In the months that followed, his nightmares became worse, he missed hospital appointments and twice tried to take his own life. It also took its toll on his relationship with his girlfriend. On New Year's Eve, he dressed in his army uniform and drove into the Pembrokeshire mountains. After recording a farewell video on his phone, the 29-year-old killed himself. His girlfriend told *Panorama*: 'I wanted to help him but I just didn't know what to do.'

His loss was compounded by the family's discovery that the names of those who kill themselves once they have returned home – in contrast to those who do so while still deployed overseas – are not recorded in the National Memorial in Staffordshire. 'They're victims of war and they should be treated exactly the same,' said Dan Collins's mother.

Most tragic of all is that the stories of Dan Collins and David Finney are not unusual. The statistics tell us that the awful toll of combat trauma is an ongoing tragedy that the military and civilian authorities are failing to adequately confront. In July 2019, the coroner for Birmingham and Solihull in the UK wrote to the National Health Service and the police to list a catalogue of failures in the treatment of veteran Dave Jukes. The 49-year-old, who had served in Iraq, Afghanistan and Bosnia, had suffered with acute depression for years, traced to his experiences in war zones. A specialist mental health team, created for the purpose of treating military veterans, had delayed seeing Mr Jukes. When he was detained by police after an incident, the coroner said, he should have been seen by a psychiatrist. But poor record-keeping, a lack of information-sharing and a shortage of funds had left Lance Corporal Jukes without help. He hanged himself. His family and campaigners for veterans' welfare saw the gaps in the system that allowed a proud serviceman to fall through the cracks. The coroner saw that others suffering with PTS could go the same way. 'In my opinion there is a risk that future deaths will occur unless action is taken,' she wrote.

So often it has fallen to grieving families and veterans themselves to lead the charge for greater understanding and action on PTS. It has driven the mission of Tony Dell and Stand Tall. The charity's symbol, the orange bolt of lightning, is a representation of the life-changing impact of that shock to the human system of trauma. 'Most Australians who have the condition have contracted it serving their country in the armed forces or helping their fellow Australians in tragedies,' Dell said. 'If left untreated it develops into deep depression and people's lives crumble. The government gives minimal support for something that is a massive problem and it is growing. We have to make people aware that it is time to do something.'

There is another front in the battle to address PTS which is often overlooked, and which impacts those who have never been anywhere near a war zone.

The sight of death and horror, emergency and trauma, fear and panic are the everyday hazards of first responders. Police officers, firefighters, paramedics, ambulance crews – the army of those in a different uniform who rush to confront danger and devastation and are also prone to facing the consequences of PTS.

A study in Australia in 2018 found that one in four former first responders reported experiences of PTS. Emergency service workers were twice as likely to have suicidal thoughts than the rest of the population and three times more likely to have drawn up a detailed suicide plan. A separate parliamentary inquiry revealed that ten per cent of serving first responders had probable PTS with one taking his or her life every six weeks. A study in the UK found that nearly one in five police officers had symptoms consistent with PTS and that some two-thirds of those suffering were completely unaware of it. The responses from more than 16,000 serving officers and operational staff revealed that 90 per cent had been exposed to trauma. In summary, the report said that overall PTS rates in law enforcement were almost five times higher than the general UK population.

Many of those who responded were suffering from 'complex PTS', a condition recognised by the World Health Organisation in which the symptoms harden through repeated trauma exposure into a chronic condition of emotional numbness and disconnection. The lead researcher, Dr Jess Miller from the University of Cambridge's Department of Sociology, said complex PTS was 'the brain's gradual maladjustment to the extraordinary'. The impact was severe. 'Relentless filing of horror and human suffering inevitably changes who we are. We can start to doubt the meaningfulness of what we do and our role in the world.' Police officers described symptoms identical to those of service personnel, the nightmares and night sweats, panic and terror. The statistics from the United States were even more stark: a national survey of thousands of police officers, paramedics, emergency medical technicians and firefighters found they were ten times more likely to attempt suicide than the general population.

Another study in the US in 2019 found that one in five female firefighters had experienced symptoms of PTS, compared to one in eight of their male colleagues. Almost a third of the female firefighters had attempted or thought about suicide. What was notable about that last statistic is that the majority of the women had seen a mental health professional, suggesting that female firefighters were more receptive to outreach efforts. The study also found that gender discrimination and harassment were likely to increase women's risk of traumatic stress or suicidal thoughts. They are findings that fit with the global picture of women's greater likelihood of suffering PTS in their lifetime.

It is a global story but, in a country blighted by the phenomenon of the mass shooting, so often on school and college campuses, American emergency workers face challenges of a different scale and texture to their British and Australian counterparts.

In December 2012, a Connecticut state trooper called Ken Dillon was among those who responded to Sandy Hook Elementary School in Newtown. A gunman had killed 26 people, 20 of them toddlers. The shooting happened on what was 'pizza Friday' at the school. Dillon told the *Washington Post*: 'When everything happened, big trays of pizza were left out on the counter in the cafeteria. Over the next week while we processed the scene it began to rot and smell really bad, and it blended with the other unfortunate smells, like blood just down the hallway, the smell of evil. After that, anytime I'd smell pizza, it would take me back to that time.' Of all the horrors he had experienced in a 30-year career, 'Sandy Hook was the straw that broke the camel's back.'

What happened to Dillon next is sadly familiar: he withdrew, he carried a gun all the time, he began drinking, his marriage fell apart and he was arrested. All the anger and torment made sense when he was diagnosed with PTS. The help he received, learning to talk about what he was feeling rather than reaching for a drink, was life-changing. 'You can't delete PTS, you're never completely cured,' he told the *Post*, 'but you can learn to combat the symptoms and triggers in a healthy way.'

A bigger problem is those who never seek help. Surveys of first responders have shown many are unwilling to seek help for fear of the negative reaction from their colleagues or superiors. The heroic image of those who face danger and save lives has been blamed for portraying as weakness any mental health issue. What Tony Dell sensed in early 1970s Australia – 'you just didn't talk about mental illness' – can be just as prevalent and damaging in the modern emergency services.

Charles Figley, the former US Marine who came through Vietnam and started a revolution in the understanding of trauma on the battlefield, also came to understand that first responders face perhaps an even greater risk of PTS than service personnel. While members of the military return from a deployment with at least some chance to decompress, he said, first responders face trauma day after day with little respite to process what they have experienced. Among those to take up the cause of first responders in Australia was Sir Angus Houston, patron of Dell's Stand Tall and the country's former Chief of the Defence Force. 'It is a very different working environment from the military but there is a high incidence of PTS and suicide risk among first responders.'

The official statistics for PTS among first responders probably only tell a fraction of the story. Not generally included are part-time workers, volunteers or those who have retired or quit through stress. The intensity of some of the traumatic experiences of first responders is also on a different scale to that of military personnel. For police officers forced to pore through evidence of child sexual abuse or review horrific terrorist content, often without any support, the long-term cost can be extreme. They also describe the feeling of responsibility to victims of crime, that they are the only hope of justice for people in desperate need. Like veterans dealing with PTS, police officers rarely report that their superiors know how to deal with prevention or cure.

But the reach of PTS has also pushed on beyond those in uniform. Just one example can be found in a study published in the *Medical Journal of Australia* in 2018. It reported that severe droughts in the country over the previous decade were creating a mental health crisis among farmers. Those aged under 35 were particularly vulnerable to the stresses of losing their jobs or income. They were also the group least likely to ask for help. For years researchers have been telling us that people living in rural areas faced a greater exposure to the possibility of traumatic events. Remoteness was known to compound the feelings of isolation. The increased chance of floods, droughts and bushfires was now found to be piling on the pressure.

Allan Sparkes – the only Australian ever to be awarded the country's highest civilian award, the Cross of Valour, and a Commendation for Brave Conduct – worked as a jackaroo, wool presser and shearer before embarking on a 20-year career as a police officer. Outwardly functional and successful, he was diagnosed with PTS after a series of high stress situations. 'I had a never-ending playing of events in my mind about the things that I had seen and been involved with at work. Whether it was during the daytime or at night, I couldn't close my eyes to go to sleep,' he wrote. He put his experience to good use. He became the deputy commissioner of the Mental Health Commission of New South Wales and an ambassador for the mental health non-profit Beyond Blue, helping those suffering mental health issues and depressions in rural parts of the country.

From the remotest parts of Australia to the most crowded of celebrity spaces, PTS is now a subject of discussion. In 2019, the singer Ariana Grande posted an image on social media purporting to show scans of her brain alongside those of a 'healthy brain' and the 'brain of a person with PTS'. It was at her concert in Manchester in 2017 that a suicide bomber killed 22 people, half of them children. She told *Elle* magazine: 'You hear about these things. You see it on the news, you tweet the hashtag. It's happened before and it'll happen again. It makes you sad, you think about it for a little and then people move on. But experiencing something like that first hand, you think of everything different.' Even if scientists doubt the theory that PTS can be diagnosed from brain scans, it was further proof of the condition's creep into the everyday.

Those who experience terrorist attacks and natural disasters up close are perhaps bound to suffer the consequences of trauma. But the acres of research into PTS has also found symptoms occurring in people who were nowhere near the action. In the era of 24-hour news coverage of major events, viewers can experience very real PTS simply from consuming wall-to-wall images of horror from thousands of miles away. A study which followed thousands of Americans after the bombing at the Boston Marathon and the mass shooting at the Pulse nightclub in Orlando in Florida in 2016 found they not only suffered distress from watching coverage at the time of the atrocity but also months later, in response to new horrors. This 'cycle of distress', according to Dr

David Spiegel, the director of Stanford University's Centre on Stress and Health, was the natural response of our brain's power of imagination. 'Exposure to trauma, even at a distance, will elicit the kind of reaction you might have if you are witnessing an event yourself,' he told the *Los Angeles Times*. There was a warning for all of us, broadcasters and viewers alike, in the level of attention we pay to collective tragedies.

Charles Figley saw a peculiar paradox in the military versus civilian occurrence of PTS, one of 'false positives and false negatives'. Those in the services often did everything they could to hide mental health challenges – many in civilian life were far quicker to seek out a diagnosis, he said.

There is no doubt that the term 'PTS' has become linguistic shorthand for even the most ephemeral of daily shocks and surprises. Like the equally careless use of the term OCD, the obsessive compulsive disorder that is often a companion condition to PTS, there is a danger of minimising the real and crippling effects on chronic sufferers of those conditions.

For a small organisation like Stand Tall, founded to increase awareness of PTS and try to nudge the authorities towards action, this explosion in the public's knowledge of the condition was a double-edged sword. Yes, awareness was growing, but where to target the charity's efforts was daunting. 'The list grew every time I looked and I panicked,' Tony Dell said. 'How was a small volunteer group going to manage this? The answer was simple: we're about awareness. We concentrate on the military, the veterans and the first responders. They are the most at risk and they have the highest profile. Any success we have with them would filter down to everyone else.' Ultimately, even that pragmatic approach would have to be reassessed and many of those living with the consequences of PTS were still feeling terribly alone.

Gwen Cherne had some early exposure to the symptoms. As a nine-year-old living in America's Midwest, she dreaded the chore of waking her dad. 'We either threw something at him or shook his foot and ran.' A veteran of the US Air Force, who carried memories of dropping bombs on Vietnamese villages, he would spring from his bed and stand as if on guard. It took Gwen years to realise that her childhood was blighted by the draining impact of PTS. 'I couldn't wait to live somewhere else,' she said. The moment of dawning came when her own marriage was also falling victim to the ravages of PTS.

She met her husband Pete in Afghanistan and moved to his native Australia. A sergeant in the special forces, who also served in Cambodia, Timor and Iraq, he suffered a stroke while deployed overseas. As he recovered at home, his mental health deteriorated. With three children to look after, Gwen describes a battle to manage the household and her husband's crippling condition. Some days she had a loving husband and a normal family life. On others, she was married to a man who was angry and short-tempered, prone to shutting down and the 'ten-metre stare', his children terrified to make a noise, the joy and happiness sucked from life. Gwen saw that he viewed life through a lens that had become distorted. There was paranoia, questioning whether there was a reason to live – things were very often black and white. 'He was fighting all the time just to be okay.' Attempts at therapy were abandoned almost before they started. 'It was all too much for him to handle.'

In February 2017, in the garage of the family home, Pete Cherne took his own life. Gwen is savagely honest about the impact of his suicide. Her life fell apart. She couldn't even bring herself to brush her teeth. 'I was horribly angry and sad, sitting on the floor of the kitchen, crying, while the kids were watching TV, my daughter asking, "Are you okay, mummy?" and me replying, "No, and I don't know when I will be."'

Gwen's salvation has come in trying to find some answers for others, working with groups like the War Widows' Guild. 'Pete would still be here with the right services and support around him. It should not be a life sentence, no one is a lost cause.' She takes issue with the oft-quoted statistic of PTS sufferers: that a third respond well to treatment, a third are struggling but okay and a third are said to be 'treatment resistant'. No one, she says, is treatment resistant. She wants defence authorities to be open to alternative therapies, with evidence for example that equine therapy and meditation is effective with PTS sufferers, and for them to take a more holistic approach. 'Old school thinking is the problem.' Awareness is important but so is service delivery, enough clinical psychiatric services, and you cannot have one without the other. 'They also need to recognise there is a critical moment when people are open to counselling, especially men.'

There have been more than enough warnings. Jesse Bird was a 32-year-old veteran of the war in Afghanistan and exhibiting, in the eyes of those close to him, the classic signs of PTS. Australia's Department of Veterans' Affairs had accepted liability for his condition but then denied his claim for financial assistance. With $5 in his bank account, he told the department he was in severe financial distress and was suicidal. Five days later he took his own life. An official inquiry found there were significant failures in the handling of his case and made 19 recommendations to prevent a repeat. Jesse's family is another that has been forced to fight and campaign for answers, for him and for thousands of others.

Marriage to a PTS sufferer gave Gwen Cherne a front row seat, just like Katie Dell and her children, to the condition's debilitating effects. Because, as Tony Dell himself admitted, his PTS was 'middle of the range' he made it through. Just like Gwen Cherne he felt a responsibility, like dozens of others who have suffered or lived with a sufferer, to keep agitating for better understanding and treatment. These small, disjointed campaigns have become the most powerful voice for veterans – 'a loud bunch of humans who never stop pushing', as Gwen Cherne described them – despite the repeated frustrations and the slow-moving machinery of officialdom.

Her belief that the families of veterans need to be included in their treatment is finally gaining traction. A societal change is also needed. 'Men still bear the burden of this in our society, it is largely still a male issue. Boys need to know that being stoic and silent is not what it means to be a man.'

12

SIXTY YEARS after Tony Dell departed England for Australia, he sat folded into the passenger seat of a small hire car, winding its way through the suburbs of Surrey. The county whose cricket team had thrilled him as a teenager with their dominance of the County Championship – Peter May, Jim Laker, Tony Lock and company winning seven titles in a row – had changed a lot in the intervening years. So too had Tony Dell and his visit to England in the summer of 2019 was about more than just nostalgia.

As it turned out, his arrival came at an uncomfortable time for an Aussie. Everyone in the country, not just cricket fans, seemed to be floating on the euphoria of seeing England snatch World Cup victory from New Zealand in the most dramatic of finals at Lord's. Savouring the rare taste of any English World Cup triumph had been made all the sweeter by the crushing defeat of Australia in the semi-final. An Aussie caught in the middle of all that was a sitting duck and the mocking messages poured in: did he know there was a didgeridoo competition he could go to watch instead of the final? The Ashes would offer some succour to all Australians later that summer but cricket was not Dell's primary business in the old country.

There was a growing restlessness, an increasing urgency, in his mid-seventies, to make his work matter. Perhaps there was a sense of time running out – certainly there was a feeling that the problem was growing bigger. Dell wanted to absorb the lessons others had learned and use them to make Stand Tall a better force for good. His native England had plenty of experience to offer.

Tyrwhitt House was built in 1870 by a London stockbroker as a country home for his wife, four children, three servants and governess. Set in 13 acres of rich Surrey countryside, with a lodge and a cottage, the house had its own colourful past. During World War Two, it was owned by a shipping company as a place to house its staff. With the war over, the company directors decided they wanted to put it to good use and offered it up to any charity which could match their 'very low' price of £11,000. The offer was spotted by a man who was working as the chauffeur for the Ex-Servicemen's Welfare Society. In their minutes, the charity recorded that it was a 'splendid property most suitable for our purpose as a curative centre. This has been confirmed by our medical men who had inspected it.' In 1946, the house, renamed in honour of the charity's president Sir Reginald Tyrwhitt, was officially opened by Princess Alice. Tyrwhitt had served in the Royal Navy in World War One and was a man with the 'knack of being not only in the midst of almost every scrap with the enemy but often responsible for starting it', according to a biographer. Newspapers of the time called him the 'storm petrel of the Navy', a reference to the seabird that hovers just above the roiling waves to feed, giving the impression of walking on water.

Decades later the Ex-Servicemen's Welfare Society had become known as Combat Stress and Tyrwhitt House remained one of its main treatment centres. Grand and red-bricked with small mock-Tudor touches, it is a reassuring and imposing presence, insulated from the roar of the M25 motorway by thick woodland. Inside its walls, it possesses a peace. Any visitor can sense the power of the place, almost a reverence for the calm and quiet, the escape it offers those in extreme need. There is a seriousness about the work that is being done.

The charity had been born in 1919. Its founders were horrified at the treatment of thousands of veterans returning from the front with what was then dismissed as shell shock. There was little sympathy from the public and almost nothing by way of support. If they weren't locked away in a psychiatric hospital they were left to suffer in silence at home. In fact, so ambivalent were the war authorities to the plight of those suffering mental illness that nine of the country's asylums were requisitioned to house the mounting number of casualties with physical injuries. It showed a disregard for the 12,000 civilian patients, many of whom had lived their whole lives in one place, and were now either returned to their families or shifted to other institutions. Staff at the time reported the upheaval as a cause of acute distress and, years later, those patients were themselves classified as war casualties. Such was the stigma of mental illness in the 1920s that the institutions were reclassified as 'war hospitals' so soldiers could be spared the perceived shame of being treated in a lunatic asylum.

The founders of the Ex-Servicemen's Welfare Society believed veterans with mental health problems could be helped to lead fulfilling lives if only they were given the right support. They saw themselves as taking a stand against the contempt and misunderstanding around mental health at the time. They started raising money to fund recuperative homes for veterans, places where they could take part in occupational activities to help them put their lives back together.

A hundred years later, on a bright summer's morning, Tony and Sally drove out from the chaos of central London to the solace of Tyrwhitt House. On the way, they passed the site of the first of the charity's recuperative homes on Putney Hill. The struggle that the Welfare Society pinpointed generations before was alive and well.

For Tony Dell, Tyrwhitt House provided the perfect model of what veterans with PTS needed most. On a tour of its facilities he was restless, partly due to the physical ailments that meant standing still for a prolonged period had become painful, partly the hyper-vigilance of the PTS sufferer who needs to keep moving. It can appear to the observer like irritation and impatience but those were not Dell's emotions at Tyrwhitt House. Instead there was a buzz, an excitement at seeing what a charity can really do in the service of veterans.

The walls are covered with the artwork of current and former patients, colourful and dramatic expressions of their experiences in war and peace. The veterans work in groups, these 'cohorts' providing encouragement and support. One veteran of the Falklands War had discovered a way to share his struggles, 37 years after coming home from combat, through poetry. The veterans are encouraged to enjoy the things on which they so often missed out: hobbies, fishing, art, cookery. The occupational therapy that was at the core of the charity's mission in 1919 is still there a hundred years on.

Tony and Sally's guide was Dr Walter Busuttil. From his native Malta, he had joined the RAF's medical branch. As a psychiatrist, he had helped rehabilitate hostages held in Beirut and veterans from the first Gulf War and had gone on to become one of the world's leading experts on PTS. He was also an old friend of Stand Tall. He had given the keynote address at the charity's forum in Brisbane in 2017. 'The problem is that veterans come and go, wars come and go and between wars everybody forgets that veterans will present with post-traumatic stress and other conditions and nobody will be there to treat them unless there is a champion around to do it,' he told them. Since 2007 Dr Busuttil had been the medical director at Combat Stress and few people in the world have his level of expertise.

Tyrwhitt House is an experiment in action and one that is apparently having success with its veterans. There is a quasi-military feel to the place so those who are there can feel comfortable talking among people with similar experiences. The treatment is intensive. 'People ask why we do it intensively,' Dr Busuttil said. 'We say, "Because it works." If you're intensively ill, you need intensive treatment.'

In the courtyard gardens, Dell stopped to take in the peace and tranquillity, at its centre a large koi carp pond. The wooden benches on the lawn were all high-backed and placed against the wall, sympathetic to the hyper-vigilance of the PTS sufferer, always looking over their shoulder.

If Combat Stress offered a vision of the way to treat damaged veterans, it also provided a lesson in the realities of life for charities today. The National Health Service of England had decided to withdraw its £3.2m injection, roughly a fifth of the charity's entire funding, and direct the money to its own new specialist service instead. It left Combat Stress to rely on individuals and corporate sponsors for cash. Within months, the charity had announced a funding crisis meant it would not be able to take any new cases in England and Wales at a time when it was receiving 2,000 referrals a year. It had already been forced into drastic staff cutbacks over the preceding years and the hopes for that new NHS-run service were not high. Sue Freeth, the charity's chief executive and one of Tony Dell's hosts on his visit to Tyrwhitt House, told the BBC that 80 per cent of the veterans who ended up at Combat Stress did so because they had not had their needs met by the NHS. 'I don't believe the NHS can pick this up,' she said. 'This is why we exist.'

Over lunch in a country pub, Dr Busittil laid out the picture he had built up over decades of treating the mental wounds of war, a complex tapestry of challenges and lessons. A student of those earliest Egyptian experiences of 'hysteria', in modern times he recognised that every theatre of war involving UK forces, from Northern Ireland to Afghanistan to Bosnia, left a different sort of trauma behind. Guerrilla warfare, hand-to-hand combat, the powerlessness of peacekeeping duties – each strained the consciousness in disparate ways.

Every veteran experienced those traumas differently. Two soldiers could live almost identical service lives and one could be crippled by what he experienced while the other was completely unaffected. Even if a diagnosis was made, assigning the wrong treatment could be worse than no treatment at all. Often the real problems only began to appear once a service member had returned to civilian life. The crutches of cheap drink, routine and mateship in the military, the things that had helped them limp through day-to-day life, were suddenly gone. A million veterans could attest to the reality of that shock to the system. At the time, the UK was even lacking the sort of basic research into the extent of military suicides within its own ranks. What other countries had managed the UK was only just beginning to address. PTS still represented a 'time bomb' of mental health problems which existing facilities might prove insufficient to meet.

Dell listened intently to Dr Busittil's expertise over that lunch. What if those kinds of residential courses, run by people who understood what veterans needed most, were more widely available? What if Dr Busittil could come again to Australia to draw powerful voices together?

His mind was buzzing as he left Surrey that day. In the week that followed he would find more to energise him. He learned about a community mental health project run by the NHS in the naval city of Portsmouth – where Dell's father once played rugby for the United Services team – which seemed to offer a genuine pathway for veterans who were otherwise at risk of being lost to the system. The model for everyone was the Patriot Support Program in the United States. Its network of 25 support centres across the country has been credited with having had extraordinary success in treating military-specific behavioural issues among veterans and their families. Critical to the Patriot mission was an anti-stigma campaign, fronted by former American football star Herschel Walker, who fought his own battles with mental illness and went on to offer emotional

Chapter 12

support to service members, veterans and their families. The power of the voice of a sports star to young men and women – his message that there is no shame in getting help – was one that Tony Dell had learned on his own journey of discovery.

The return visits to England in his advancing years also tweaked the nerve of nostalgia. Decades after he had played as a child on its idyllic beaches, Dell went back to his home town of Highcliffe. A photo shows him standing outside the prefab bungalow where his own story had begun. Who could have predicted the path he would have taken in life from those childhood days? There was the pond in the garden, the walk down the lane where he had once set the gorse bushes alight. 'You could see in his eyes he loved it,' said Sally. He journeyed back to Cardiff too, much changed from the place he had left to set sail with his family for a new and very different life. These moments brought the more mellow, reflective Tony Dell to the fore, the man who openly admitted weeping during a soppy movie, not the gruff and troubled war veteran who could be impatient and cutting. He talked of his relationships with parents and siblings, the good bits and the bad, and where life's journey had taken him.

Those visits to the UK also revealed a final, strange irony about Dell's life story. It was only when he realised that he needed a new passport to make a trip that he legally became an Australian citizen. Yes, remarkably, after more than 50 years of life in Australia, serving the country in war and peace, it was only in his seventies that he finally became a fair dinkum Aussie. The only times he cheers for England these days? When they're playing in the football World Cup.

In those advancing years, Dell reflected on the people who had meant most to him in his life. He talked of the 'heroes' he looked up to, who inspired him to try to be a better person. The first was Jim Monteith, his company commander in Vietnam, a man of calm, control and leadership. 'I never once saw him angry,' Dell said. 'He was a man's man and every member of Charlie Company looked up to him.'

Next came Greg Chappell. In his first year as Queensland captain, one of the greatest batsmen his country has ever produced was often frustrated that those around him could not rise to the standards he expected. 'No wonder we called him God,' said Dell. 'Not to his face though.' Chappell adapted and mastered captaincy and remained a friend to Dell through the good times and the bad.

Another sporting god was Sir Alex Ferguson. As a child Dell had idolised the youthful and exuberant Manchester United side crafted by Sir Matt Busby. Like a generation of young fans, he was devastated by the loss of so many of that team in the air crash at Munich in 1958. Ferguson's own careful nurturing of young talent at United and the glittering success that followed thrilled Dell all over again. It was Ferguson's never-say-die leadership though, that inspired him the most. 'They saved or won more than 160 matches in the final few minutes. Like them, I will never die wondering.'

Some of those heroes were less high-profile. Dell played a lot of cricket with Peter Evans at Eastern Suburbs in Brisbane. In Evans he saw a leader who would end up backing him 'verbally, emotionally and financially through thick and thin for nearly 40 years'.

Walking the corridors of power with Sir Angus Houston had given Dell the nerve to continue Stand Tall's work. He had been the man who also got Dell over the shyness to tell his own story in the hope it would inspire others.

Dell saw elements of all those men in his last hero, his son Barney. 'I have watched him grow into the sort of person every father wants.'

The part the rest of his family played in a life of intense highs and lows, sadness and joy, moved him to deeper reflection. His father Ross, a probable sufferer of PTS himself: 'He never once talked to me about his war. I wish he had.' His mother Barbara, who had taught him compassion and family values. His brothers Chris and Jonny, both long gone, who had been his antithesis, softer and more creative. 'I've missed them so much.' His own children, Barney, Josie and Minnie: 'I went missing from you and your mother for some time but I'm glad we found each other again.' His final thought was for Sally, the person he had 'loved the most in my lifetime came back into my life after 40 years and I found the real meaning of that word once again'.

As Dell reflected on his own life, there were plenty of others who had their own thoughts and theories on what had become of that young cricketer and soldier.

His friend Greg Chappell remained in no doubt that Dell and Australia were robbed of a far more significant cricket career. 'He was a quality bowler and, in different circumstances, could have had a very different career. His name would have been spoken very differently. If he didn't have the misfortune of going to Vietnam, it could have made a big difference to his life and certainly his cricket career.'

In the cricketing landscape of the mid-70s, Chappell thought, Dell could have featured in Australia's tours to the West

Indies and England. The pitches and conditions in England in particular would have suited Dell's height and swing, Chappell said. Dell was still only 30 when Australia toured England in 1975. Two years later, the dawn of Kerry Packer's World Series Cricket had created a split in the sport and tested Australia's reserves of bowling quality. Chappell certainly believed that Dell's career would have benefitted from accepting one of those offers to play county cricket back in England in his early days, perhaps alongside Barry Richards with his native Hampshire. Over the years Dell has given various explanations for turning down the chance and, whatever the truth, the fact remains he stayed in Australia. There were many regrets for Chappell about his friend and former team-mate. 'It was sad in hindsight that what happened to him in Vietnam might have curtailed a cricket career.'

Other friends agree. 'I was stunned when he walked away because he could have gone a lot further,' said his old schoolfriend Greg Delaney. Dell himself was unwilling to venture too far into the territory of regret but, for whatever reason, he appeared at times to have developed a love-hate relationship with the game. 'A couple of years ago I was talking to him and he said he didn't watch the cricket anymore,' said Delaney. 'I don't know whether that was bullshit or fair dinkum.'

Not all of those who have been there throughout Dell's life are as convinced that his experiences in Vietnam fully explain what happened to his personality. One lifelong friend, who preferred to remain anonymous in expressing this sentiment, believed the instability was there before he went to war. 'I think he would always have ended up being a bit depressed as a person. What

Chapter 12

happened to him in Vietnam probably hastened or worsened what was always going to happen to him.' It was a controversial opinion, he accepted, and would probably prove an unpopular one with the man himself.

What all those friends agreed on was the improvement to Dell's life brought about by the presence of Sally by his side and the work of Stand Tall ahead of him.

Like many anxiety disorders, PTS is cruelly effective at robbing the sufferer of enjoyment and experience. Distract the brain from the pain, secure some short-term relief, move on. In Tony Dell's case it has meant that little of his cricket career remains in the memory. But the understanding that came with his diagnosis has finally allowed him to piece together some of life's experiences. He revealed how it all comes full circle in an ANZAC Day speech at the Greenslopes Hospital in Brisbane.

In the 1960s, he told his audience, he and his friends used to hang out at the nearby bowling alley, clutching supplies and hoping for word of the latest party populated by nurses. His first serious girlfriend was the daughter of a bookmaker who lived just up the road. In the 1970s, his father-in-law Hector Spring, veteran of Lancaster bomber raids in Europe in World War Two, had breathed his last in the hospital's old wooden Queenslander-style buildings. Dell returned to the hospital for regular skin cancer check-ups, and to take part in a groundbreaking new study into PTS being carried out at the Gallipoli Medical Research Foundation. On that day, when Australians reflect on those who have given so much in combat, Dell told the audience: 'There is a little phrase that is used many times over at this time of year and it could become a little bit cliché. I hope it doesn't ever lose its meaning. "Lest we forget". I can tell you now the prevalence of post-traumatic stress disorder in this country will never let us forget the ravages of war.'

Five years later, thousands of miles away, on a train rattling through the commuter belt west of London, those sentiments were still the foundation of Tony Dell's life. He gazed out at the passing English scene, the physical toll of a sporting career he could barely remember making life increasingly uncomfortable. He reflected that many veterans had chosen another way out of the suffering. To him, suicide or drink had never been an option, just ploughing on with what had become his life's work.

On a sweltering Wednesday in July in the summer of 2019, he was sitting at a picnic table under the trees on the boundary at Windsor Cricket Club in Berkshire. There are few other cricket grounds in England that can boast a backdrop like it: the stately Windsor Castle watches down from a hilltop to the south, a lazy loop of the River Thames sweeps around the other three sides of the ground.

He was there to watch a few overs of a match between a team made up of English 'Barmy Army' cricket fans and youngsters touring with the academy run by former Australia bowler Jason Gillespie. Dell has already walked away from a discussion with one of the scorers about batting techniques of the Australians at the World Cup. He now grumbles about the bowlers on display at Windsor. Not enough front arm. Too chest-on. These are familiar gripes to anyone who has been on the end of a Dell sermon on the problems of modern, particularly Australian, cricket. It has even got him blocked from an official email server or two. As Greg Chappell said: 'He is forthright and he's ruffled a few feathers and perhaps he's coloured the way people react to him. He feels very strongly but I don't think people are particularly interested in what players from the past think about how the game is played.' Delaney put it more bluntly: 'He gets the shits up with the cricket hierarchy.'

Dell had flown those 10,000 miles to the country of his birth to promote the work that has dominated his life for the last decade. 'Stand Tall 4 PTS' was founded with the aim of giving every Australian a clear understanding of the condition and a respect for those affected by it. Dell wanted to shatter the misconceptions, remove the stigma and increase access to professional support for sufferers. To do this, he reckoned, he needed to put pressure on governments to find the money for meaningful research and treatment. But PTS is not an Australian problem alone. Picking the brains of those involved in research and care around the world would inform the way forward. Dell wanted the best minds around his table.

Cricket was one way to get attention and spread the message on that visit to England. Plans had faltered for a Twenty20 tournament featuring a men's and women's defence team, one from the charity Help for Heroes as well as the Barmy Army and their Australian counterparts, the 'Fanatics'. For all the boisterous efforts of the Barmy Army and Gillespie's under-19s playing in honour of Stand Tall, there was a palpable disappointment for Dell.

As the jets climb out of Heathrow Airport into the clear blue sky above, Dell pondered the future. He remained upbeat about the work of Stand Tall but the impatience and frustration at the authorities dragging their heels, all the talk and no action in his eyes, was never far away. 'I'm pretty certain we've made a difference to hundreds of people's lives,' he said. 'I get phone calls and texts saying: "Thank you for what you are doing."'

The charity had been evolving. As the reach of PTS stretched further into society, so the need for help and understanding grew. Dell was annoyed that so much good work was being wasted as researchers and academics around the world appeared to operate in silos. The lack of coordination or sharing of the knowledge was hampering progress. Those researchers and academics presented their findings to each other or published the results in scientific journals but the wider population remained in the dark. All the while the success rate in treating veterans had barely shifted. The need was for an overarching strategic direction to harness all of that work and the answer was 'One Voice for Mental Trauma'. Dell's Stand Tall joined forces with other veterans who had experience at the coal face of PTS to try to bring together the knowledge being collected around the world and make a difference on the ground. 'Research is extremely important but we think it takes time to undertake, to prove and to implement this information into practice. Meanwhile, the suicide rate does not slow down.' But hopes of holding a forum, as with much of what the world was planning in 2020, were dealt a crippling blow by the coronavirus pandemic. There was some dark irony that a global health catastrophe would create a whole new batch of mental health challenges while choking off the very effort to find answers.

Dell was not alone in his frustrations. Gwen Cherne, who had begun her own campaign after the death of her husband Pete, saw simple lessons. Every pregnant woman who goes to hospital, she said, is aware of the risk of post-natal depression and the services available to help. The same should be true for men and women going into war zones: the risks are understood and the support services are actively promoted. There needs to be awareness but also enough clinicians to provide those services.

Dell's own push for action continued to grow. 'One Voice' became part of the global 'Change Direction' initiative to change the culture surrounding mental health. Inspired by a discussion at a White House conference in 2013, it drew on the likes of former First Lady Michelle Obama and actor Richard Gere and pulled together the public and private sector and non-profit organisations. 'Change Direction' called on the public to be aware of the five signs that might reveal friends, neighbours, relatives or colleagues were suffering emotional pain: personality changes, uncharacteristic anger, anxiety, agitation or moodiness, withdrawal or isolation from other people, neglect of self-care or engaging in risky behaviour, a sense of hopelessness or being overwhelmed. These were the things that groups like Stand Tall had been hammering away at for years and, now, this was the global, high-profile, joined-up effort Dell had long believed was necessary.

Dell, though, like all of us, is limited by the time we have on the planet. 'It would probably cease to exist if he fell off the perch tomorrow,' Sally said. Few people had the vision, the passion, the experience, the connections, the creativity, the ideas – some realistic, others less so – to carry on what Dell had started. She lamented that some had taken him for a ride, tried to get something out of a man who was very trusting. 'The spirit will be willing forever but, physically ...' she trailed off.

He had ploughed much of his own money into Stand Tall yet finding new sources of funding, reaching out in the digital age, had become increasingly difficult. Every new initiative was a spark of hope, a new avenue to be explored, the never-say-die attitude.

'It is one man, that's what Stand Tall is, it is Tony Dell. He calls it his obligation, not just a passion. I don't know what he would do if he didn't do this. It has done some amazing things. If it disappears, it disappears, it will have served a purpose for him in giving his life meaning.'

Tony Dell, the English boy who grew up to fight in a war for Australia and play cricket for his adopted homeland against his original one, had already led a life more fulfilling than many. His remaining ambition was a simple one. 'The more I talk about it, the more that people see that it's not just them going through it. The more it can encourage them to talk, then I have done something worthwhile. It is my therapy. Let's see what we can do to help others.'

Bibliography

Beaumont, Joan, *Broken Nation* (Sydney: Allen & Unwin, 2013).

Caulfeld, Michael, *The Vietnam Years* (Sydney: Hachette Australia, 2007).

Dean, Eric, *Shook Over Hell* (London: Harvard University Press, 1997).

Edwards, Peter, Australia and the Vietnam War (Sydney: NewSouth, 2014)

Figley, Charles, *Stress Disorders Among Vietnam Veterans* (Psychology Press, 1978)

O'Brien, Tim, *The Things They Carried* (New York: Houghton Mifflin, 1990).

Shay, Jonathan, *Achilles in Vietnam* (New York: Simon & Schuster, 2010).